Y0-BDD-703

Praise for
More Beauty, Less Beast

"*More Beauty, Less Beast* will revolutionize your thinking about the who, what, and how of beauty and fashion. My friend Debora Coty is funny, insightful, and beautiful inside and out. And you are, too!"
–Martha Bolton, Emmy and Dove nominated writer,
author of 84 books of humor, and former staff writer for Bob Hope

"Embrace the realities of flab, chuckle at the dubious joys of growing older, and exercise those abs with giggles as you read a much-needed reminder that God gives us every tool for true beauty and doesn't mind if we want to accessorize anyway."
–Cindy Sigler Dagnan, speaker and author of
Hot Chocolate for Couples. www.cindydagnan.com

"*More Beauty, Less Beast* is both spiritual retreat and much needed makeover, complete with one of my favorite aerobic activities—belly laughing!"
–Shellie Rushing Tomlinson, Belle of All Things Southern
and author of *Sue Ellen's Girl Ain't Fat, She Just Weighs Heavy!*

"Deb Coty is funny and wise. This is my favorite combination in any human being. Even better when you find it in a writer."
–Rachel St. John-Gilbert, author of
Laugh Yourself to Sleep and *The Well-Lived Laugh*

© 2012 by Debora M. Coty

Print ISBN 978-1-61626-347-8

eBook Editions:
Adobe Digital Edition (.epub) 978-1-60742-796-4
Kindle and MobiPocket Edition (.prc) 978-1-60742-797-1

All rights reserved. No part of this publication may be reproduced or transmitted for commercial purposes, except for brief quotations in printed reviews, without written permission of the publisher.

Churches and other noncommercial interests may reproduce portions of this book without the express written permission of Barbour Publishing, provided that the text does not exceed 500 words or 5 percent of the entire book, whichever is less, and that the text is not material quoted from another publisher. When reproducing text from this book, include the following credit line: "From *More Beauty, Less Beast*, by Debora M. Coty, published by Barbour Publishing, Inc. Used by permission."

Scripture quotations marked NIV are taken from the HOLY BIBLE, NEW INTERNATIONAL VERSION®. NIV®. Copyright © 1973, 1978, 1984, 2011 by Biblica, Inc.™ Used by permission. All rights reserved worldwide.

Scripture quotations marked CEV are from the Contemporary English Version, Copyright © 1991, 1992, 1995 by American Bible Society. Used by permission.

Scripture quotations marked KJV are taken from the King James Version of the Bible.

Scripture quotations marked NKJV are taken from the New King James Version®. Copyright © 1982 by Thomas Nelson, Inc. Used by permission. All rights reserved.

Scripture quotations marked NASB are taken from the New American Standard Bible, © 1960, 1962, 1963, 1968, 1971, 1972, 1973, 1975, 1977, 1995 by The Lockman Foundation. Used by permission.

Scripture quotations marked MSG are taken from *THE MESSAGE*. Copyright © by Eugene H. Peterson, 1993, 1994, 1995, 1996, 2000, 2001, 2002. Used by permission of NavPress Publishing Group.

Scripture quotations marked NLT are taken from the *Holy Bible*. New Living Translation, copyright © 1996, 2004, 2007 by Tyndale House Foundation. Used by permission of Tyndale House Publishers, Inc. Carol Stream, Illinois 60188. All rights reserved.

Published in association with the literary agency of WordServe Literary Group, Ltd., www.wordserveliterary.com.

Cover illustration: Violet Iemay—agoodson.com

Published by Barbour Publishing, Inc., P.O. Box 719, Uhrichsville, Ohio 44683, www.barbourbooks.com

Our mission is to publish and distribute inspirational products offering exceptional value and biblical encouragement to the masses.

Member of the
Evangelical Christian
Publishers Association

Printed in the United States of America.

Debora M. Coty

More Beauty Less Beast

Transforming
Your Inner Ogre

BARBOUR
PUBLISHING

To my sister and hero,
Cynthia Ellen Mitchell Hardee,
whose beauty—both inside and out—
has touched more lives than she'll ever know.

Acknowledgments

I am passionately grateful for the invaluable assistance of
beautiful souls who helped make this book live, breathe,
and fight dragons (I mean ogres):

Kelly McIntosh, my sweet and ever-encouraging editor at Barbour
Publishing. Your inner loveliness lights up my literary life!

WordServe's Greg Johnson, literary agent extraordinaire; you are
so beautiful to meeeeee... (can you hear me singing, bro?).

Chuck Coty, my extraordinarily patient husband and bottomless
source of Bible knowledge. You're like my mascara, dearest! You
make me look better than I really am, and I'd never dream of going
anywhere without you!

Beloved friends and family who shared the beauty (sometimes
amid the ashes) of their own life stories. Please forgive me if I
accidentally omit someone: Cricket Boyer, Cookie Gray, Linda G.,
Mike M., Liz G., Leslie R., Betty and Jim, Kim R., Cheryl J., Debbie
B., Teresa R., and Cherylyn B.

Most of all, I give every smidgeon of credit and praise to slayer of
beasts and source of all beauty, Papa God, who is more than able
to do exceeding, abundantly, beyond all that any of us have ever
imagined (see Ephesians 3:20). To Him be the glory forever and
ever!

Contents

Introduction

Do you, like me, have a hard time keeping a muzzle on your snarling inner beast? Does your carefully fashioned facade hide what's really underneath the surface—a bubbling cauldron of leaking guilt, or maybe self-esteem that's just north of pond scum? Are you just *over* busyness and chronic fatigue stealing life's beauty from you?

Well, if so, you're not alone. I get you, sister. And so do a multitude of others.

I'm so glad you've joined us on our quest to discover God's standard of beauty. Together we'll explore the reasons makeup, hairstyles, and clothes hold power over us; how experiencing true beauty is interconnected with a rested, open spirit; and why it is we sometimes sabotage ourselves and miss both.

We'll discover the difference between ice-cream guilt and I-scream guilt, how *not* to feel invisible, and practical ways to log on to our spiritual search engine. We'll learn how to recognize ogre escape symptoms, how to realize that we're not defined by our mistakes, and how to be made lovely and new by the slipcover for the soul—forgiveness.

And the next time we get angry enough to barf, we'll actually do it! (Using the BARF response technique: Back off, Admit, Redirect, and Forgive.) Our quest will cover outer and inner beauty, fruit of the Spirit underwear, and how to beautify our world. We'll even get inside-out bad habit flips through "Taming the Beast" application questions at the end of each short chapter.

So step with me into the Divine Beauty Salon, girlfriend. Take my hand (don't worry, my beastie claws are retracted) and get ready for not just a makeover, but a transformation. For only when you feel truly loved can you feel truly lovely, and the Lover of Your Soul has a styling chair ready and waiting just for you.

Section 1:

Outer Beauty

Appearance is on the top of
most women's priority list.
And rightly so—
we are reflections of our Creator.
But who decides what's
beautiful and what's not?

*What matters is not your outer appearance—
the styling of your hair, the jewelry
you wear, the cut of your clothes—
but your inner disposition.*

1 PETER 3:3–4 MSG

CHAPTER 1

Beauty Can Be Such a Crock

(Judging by Appearance)

Like a gold ring in a pig's snout is a
beautiful face on an empty head.

PROVERBS 11:22 MSG

Okay, girlfriend, spill:

- ☐ 1. Do you currently own more than three bottles of skin moisturizer?
- ☐ 2. Have you weighed yourself within the last week?
- ☐ 3. Have you ever been embarrassed by your pants size?
- ☐ 4. Do you enjoy reading fashion magazines?
- ☐ 5. Are you unhappy with your figure?
- ☐ 6. Is there a celebrity you wish you looked more like?
- ☐ 7. Do you own more than four tubes of lipstick?
- ☐ 8. Have you used more than three different hair products during the past month?
- ☐ 9. Do you feel self-conscious if you leave the house without your makeup?
- ☐ 10. Have you had or ever considered having cosmetic surgery?
- ☐ 11. Do you have your nails done more than twice a year?
- ☐ 12. Have you bought a new outfit during the last month?

If you answered yes to three or more of these questions, I think it's safe to say that you, like most women, have an active interest in your appearance. You've actually invested in beautification with your money, time, and effort. You want to shine, baby, and positively influence the way others think of you.

Well, I'm here to tell you there's nothing wrong with that.

The God of beauty created us women with an appreciation for beauty in our spirits. We're drawn to beauty—a glorious sunset, the tiny fingers of a newborn baby, sunlight sparkling like jewels on a lake, snowcapped mountaintops. We yearn to drink it in as it captivates our minds, nourishes our souls, even inspires our hearts. We want to experience beauty—to enjoy it, create it, *be* it. So we devote our energies, resources, and time to making ourselves more beautiful. Or at least how we *think* others perceive beauty.

But you and I both know that perceptions can be deceiving, especially when we judge solely by appearance. Need proof? What are your first thoughts when you encounter a dirty, unkempt bag lady shuffling down the street? How about the highly fashionable socialite appearing in this year's Prada? The tattooed teenage boy in his hulking monster truck, cutting you off in traffic? The meticulously groomed young man looking svelte in a lab coat? The six-foot model with her Botox-perfect complexion and surgically enhanced DD chest, posing for an advertisement? Or the grossly overweight man crowding you in the elevator?

Even when we know better, we still tend to make snap judgments based on empirical evidence. We dis the one but respect the other before giving either a chance to prove him- or herself beneath the outside layer.

We don't bother to remove the wrapping paper before deciding whether we like the contents of the package.

Thankfully, Papa God doesn't think that way when He looks at us. "The LORD does not look at the things people look at. People look at the outward appearance, but the LORD looks at the heart" (1 Samuel 16:7 NIV). The gifts the Lord specifically gives each of us are rarely on the surface. He's lovingly nestled virtues like discernment, kindness, or graciousness within our character. (We'll talk more about inner beauty later.)

So why do we spend so much time rewrapping and redecorating our customized gift package? Because we want to *feel* better. Our Creator wired us so that how we look affects how we feel. There's no denying it. When we know we look good, we feel good! It's been that way from the beginning. I'll bet Eve turned the Garden of Eden upside down searching for the perfect fig leaf and coordinated banana frond purse for the first fabulous ensemble.

Hey, don't you like to strut your stuff when you're sizzling?

I just adore showing off my newly polished toenails. I do, indeed, feel pretty, oh so pretty. . .and I'm not above whirling about, flaunting my flashy feminine footsies under the wrinkled noses of whomever I can corner. I get giddy with girly-ness!

Well, what woman doesn't want to feel attractive, charming, fascinating?

When we feel pretty, we get a natural high, a boost in self-confidence. When we're at our physical best, our spirit soars and our attitude about beauty—I call this our *beaut-i-tude*—leaps into I-want-more mode. So we shop, highlight, polish, peel, gloss, and push-up to get more. The problem arises when, like with any other addiction, we can't stop.

My friend Lydia, who is beauty queen gorgeous, found out the hard way how obsession with appearance can have disastrous consequences.

One day in 2004, Lydia began experiencing a low-grade fever and blurred vision. Within hours, a rare virus had caused complete blindness in her left eye and a 50 percent loss of vision in her right eye. The consequences were thick glasses and a host of steroid-induced symptoms.

Lydia's long, lustrous chestnut hair fell out in clumps, resulting in her using a wig even all these years later. Her slim figure ballooned, and her skin aged so badly, Lydia says, "Even my knees wrinkled—nothing was untouched."

How did Lydia, the enviable woman with perfect nails, flawless makeup, and size 4 designer clothing—the woman whose self-esteem had always been wrapped up in glamour—deal with the sudden loss of the image for which she'd been so admired?

"My looks were the most important thing to me—my husband says that I was one of the vainest people he's ever met. And then God took my looks away. I was intensely angry at first and miserable. But it's a funny thing—I've grown closer to Him in my dependency. Now I don't have to worry or think about myself so much. I can focus on more important things, like reaching out to others."

Yes, when we're preoccupied with ourselves, we're distracted from our one true focus: our God and Savior, Jesus Christ, and the *people* He has brought into our lives to be our special ministry. Our passion is directed inward rather than outward. Our bodies become like a god to us. But our Creator had something very important to say about that: "You shall have no other gods before Me" (Exodus 20:3 NKJV), the very first of the Ten Commandments.

No other gods. Just the one true capitalized God. Jehovah. Yahweh. I Am. Not cheap fake gods like "Debbie Is," or "Debbie's All That," or "Debbie Wants to Be."

Just the other day I had a standoff with these false gods that I inadvertently worship. As I stood beside my car, filling my gas tank after sweating off my makeup on the tennis court, I glanced up and caught sight of my reflection in the side window. Gasp! Was that really *me*? It didn't look like the me in my head—the self-image I'd had for the past decade.

I mean, how often do we *really* look at ourselves? For me, it's just a casual glance in a mirror a few times a day to make sure I don't have spinach between my teeth or my hair isn't sticking out like a static-charged kitten. But there in the glaring light of day, every naked wrinkle (I call them laugh footprints), eye bag, gaping pore, discolored blemish, and saggy jowl showed up horrifyingly clear. My self-perception obviously hadn't marched to the same drummer as Father Time.

Talk about a harsh reality check. My hand flew to my cheek. "Am I. . .am I. . .*ugly*?"

My mind flashed back to a defining moment years before, one that I shared in my book *Mom NEEDS Chocolate*. As a chubby twelve-year-old, self-conscious about my changing body and feeling exposed to the world in my bathing suit, I stood cowering on the high dive at the public pool. Afraid to jump, I backed away from the edge of the platform, accidentally bumping an older girl waiting in line behind me.

"Go on, jump!" she snapped.

I hesitated, trembling.

She shook her head with contempt. "You shouldn't be up here. You're chicken. You're fat. And you're *ugly*."

I jumped. It was the only way to hide the tears.

Fast-forward forty years and I'm standing in a gas station, still struggling with the same ugliness issue. But now I know that viewing myself as ugly is a slap in the face to my Creator, who made me in His image. If I'm ugly, what does that make Him?

After the initial shock (and a little chocolate comfort food), I truly didn't *feel* ugly. Despite the cold hard evidence glaring back at me, I actually started to feel, well, beautiful. It was then I realized that beauty is a linear process. The process goes like this:

1. Because of the affirmation I receive from my close relationship with Papa God, I feel loved.
2. Because I know I'm loved, I feel valued.
3. Because I rest in the assurance that I'm valued, I feel beautiful.

Yes, that's right. At the risk of your thinking I'm a blind, arrogant diva, I'll say it again: *I feel beautiful.*

And you can feel beautiful, too—despite any cold hard evidence you *think* you see in the mirror! That "evidence" is just a crock of lies the world imposes on you as its unattainable standard of beauty. *Nobody* is naturally flaw-free, wrinkle-free, freckle-free, or sag-less.

This is your therapy for today: Repeat after me, "Mirrors are stupid!"

No, really, they are. Stupid, stupid, stupid. Mirrors don't *know* anything. They only tell us what we tell them to tell us. And *that* info is based on what others insist is acceptable or unacceptable through magazines, TV, infomercials, the Internet, and movies. And remember, they're all trying to sell something!

How boring would we be without laugh-till-you-cry lines? And kindness crinkles? And love handles? And a little jowl jiggle to remind us of the scoop of moose tracks we shared with that distraught friend?

That's beauty by God's measuring standard, sister. All other rulers are just wood.

Wrinkles should merely indicate where smiles have been.

Mark Twain

Taming the Beast

1. What makes your beaut-i-tude (attitude about beauty) soar to 9 on a 1 to 10 scale? Art? Music? Nature? Shopping? New shoes?
2. It's been said, "Beauty may be skin deep, but ugly goes clear to the bone." Can you think of a time when you felt misjudged by your appearance? How about a time you misjudged someone else?
3. Are there any false beauty gods you've been worshipping lately? Don't sit there and shake your head, darlin'—dig deep and 'fess up. If I'm going to be *real*, you are, too!

CHAPTER 2

Flab Is Drab

(Keeping Fit)

*Workouts in the gymnasium are useful, but a disciplined life in
God is far more so, making you fit both today and forever.
You can count on this. Take it to heart.*

1 TIMOTHY 4:8–9 MSG

The day I'd dreaded had arrived. My annual physical. Shivering in my
flimsy paper gown, I waited in the tiny sterile room for my gynecologist.
Aack! I couldn't believe I'd gained another two pounds since last year. It
was the same story for the last fifteen years —only a couple of pounds
each year, but it had sure added up. And I felt that extra thirty pounds
in my creaky knees, painful feet, and difficulty catching my breath. It
seemed as if my weight—and health—were spiraling out of control.

"Hi there, Deb." Doc bustled in, staring at my chart. He glanced
up at me and then back down, flipping pages.

"Are you taking that calcium supplement I prescribed?"

"Sure." *When I remember. Which is every other Thursday if it's not
raining.*

"How about the colonoscopy? Have you had that yet?"

"Um, not yet." *Yeah, right. When Mars aligns with Uranus.*

"And the bone density test? Got it scheduled?"

"Soon." *Don't hold your breath, Doc. I'm waaay too busy.*

"I see your weight has hit an all-time high; what's up with that?"

"Beats me." (Pause for teeth-gnashing moment.) "I'm not eating

any differently than I always have." *Except for those triple-chunk breakfast brownies.*

He put the chart down and gazed hard into my eyes.

"You're fifty now, Debbie; likely more than halfway through your life. You only have one go at this. Don't you think it's time you took responsibility for your health before it's too late?"

Too late? Gulp.

I hadn't thought of it that way. I had simply been living my frenzied life like every other woman I knew—on the run, taking care of my family with little thought for myself, grabbing whatever was easiest to eat, and squeezing in a little exercise once in a while as time and leftover energy permitted.

But Doc had gotten my attention. It was time to put on my big girl panties and accept responsibility for myself. *My* weight. *My* health. If I wouldn't, who would?

So began my adventure into recapturing control of my health. No doubt about it—getting fit is hard work. Staying fit can be even harder with today's rushing, gushing, Lycra-tight schedules. I've discovered that the only way to make new, healthful habits stick is to stick with them long enough to make them habits.

May I share with you a few important things I've learned on my journey back to health? Well, sister, hard as it is, let's face facts:

1. It costs big bucks to pack extra pounds. Researchers found that with all things considered (clothes, sick days, food costs, etc.), the annual cost of being overweight for women is $524 and a whopping $4,879 if you're considered obese (40 percent or more over your ideal body weight based on height, gender, and age).[1]

2. For every 2.2 pounds gained after age eighteen, women's odds of surviving past seventy drop 5 percent. Prevalent killer diseases are cancer, heart disease, stroke, and diabetes.[2]

3. Abdominal fat is scary. If your waist circumference is larger than 35 inches, regardless of your health or weight, you have twice the risk of dying prematurely.[3]

4. Like me, many women add several pounds per year as they age. I call this "boo baggage." It sneaks up on you until one day when you least expect it, twenty to thirty rotten, stinking pounds jump out and yell, "Boo!" For non-dieters over age forty and of average weight, an hour of moderate activity is required *each day* to avoid collecting boo baggage. Examples of moderate activity are brisk walking, tennis doubles, leisurely bicycling, and golfing.[4] I don't think nervous breakdowns or frenzied shopping count.

5. Within one year, women receiving chemotherapy treatment for breast cancer can exchange muscle for fat that's equivalent to ten years of normal aging.[5]

6. If you spend eight or more hours per day sitting in front of a computer (or TV), the fat-burning chemicals in your body are diminished by 50 percent.[6]

Ay-yi-yi! So what's a crazy-busy girl to do? Well, first off, consider this: The time you can't afford to spend on fitness now will sooner or later be consumed by illness. It's pay now or pay later. Which bill would you rather cough up?

I decided to pay now, sucked it up, and lost forty pounds (which I'll discuss more in chapter 3). Here are some fitness tips I've found helpful and relatively simple to implement:

- Ban cigarettes. If you've ever watched a loved one wither away with emphysema or lung cancer, you know why quitting is essential.
- Step smart. Movement is medicine. Walk, jog, or run at a pace brisk enough that you can still speak, but not sing, for a *minimum* of thirty minutes, three times weekly (forty-five minutes for five days is even better). I make mine a prayer walk and improve my spiritual health along with the physical!
- Get that rear in gear. To fight CCCB (computer chair cauliflower buns), take frequent movement breaks every half hour you sit: Stand, stretch, squeeze your buns, rise to your toes, do ten jumping jacks. Don't sacrifice buns of steel for buns of dough.

And *while you're typing*:

1. Stretch your legs straight ahead while flexing and extending your ankles; then slowly bend alternate knees like you're walking. Feel the hamstring stretch of the extended leg? Good! Do it again.
2. Become a hovercraft. Place a foot on either side of your chair and lift your derriere by shifting your weight onto your thighs (great way to tone them up!). Hover, much like "the position" you assume at a public toilet, until you feel the burn, baby.
3. Shift your weight onto your right bun while stretching your left leg out to the left side of your chair; squeeze your left bun; repeat toward the right. This is what I call "dog at a fire hydrant." But resist the urge.

- Don't take TV sitting down! Get that carcass off the sofa and watch from an exercise bike or treadmill. No equipment handy? No

problem! Jump rope, do sit-ups, sing the "Head, Shoulders, Knees, and Toes" song during commercials; become a human pretzel—don't waste this ideal waist-reducing time. Actively convert those carbs, fats, and sugars into aches, pains, and ice packs.

- Avoid the fast lane. Pack your lunch and healthy snacks. Did you know that each drive-through foray adds an average of 500 calories to your day? Studies have found that gals scarfing fast food more than twice a week are ten pounds heavier than those who only rarely indulge.[7]

- Get food out of sight, out of mind, and off the behind. Portion control is crucial. When dining out, box half your meal before you even begin so you can clean your plate guilt-and-temptation free. I save half my meal for the next day—the food tastes better when I know I'm only getting half the calories and it gives me something yummy to look forward to!

- Sip, nip, and dip. Eat and drink slowly (you'll feel full faster), share dessert (a few bites will satisfy your sweet tooth and sharing will create more fun with the girls or intimacy with the spouse), and have your salad dressing on the side (dipping each bite, instead of coating each shred of lettuce, saves a slew of calories).

- Stop in the name of Dove! When snacking, set out only the portion you intend to devour; then stop! Don't allow yourself a second visit to the box, bag, or fridge. Remember, girlfriend, impulse nibbling is ab-flab's BFF.

- Be picky. To ward off obesity, cancer, and heart disease, as well as reduce wrinkles, muscle soreness, and fatigue, add antioxidants to your diet, such as nuts, papaya, spinach, chicken breasts, Brussels sprouts, and. . .wait for it. . .dark chocolate!

- Get smart! Did you know that with apps like RunKeeper,

Cyclemeter, MyTracks, Lose It!, and GymTechnik you can turn your smart phone into your very own personal fitness trainer?[8] Become a pro! Be proactive and productive, but never prosaic (means dull or unimaginative!).

So did you hear about the nutty nutrition professor who experimented with a "convenience store diet," in which he ate only junk food for eight weeks?[9] In place of balanced meals, Mark Haub of Kansas State University consumed packaged goodies like Doritos, Twinkies, Little Debbie's, and Oreos, but strategically limited his intake to 1,800 calories daily without altering his regular exercise routine.

The result? Girl, get ready to screech. *He lost 27 pounds.*

There's no actual data on the health detriments of such a diet (and you can bet there would be long-term), but there's no mistaking that quantity—regardless of quality—of calories has a direct influence on weight management. Bottom line: If you burn up more calories than you swallow, you lose weight. Whether those calories come from carrots or carrot cake.

And listen, don't ignore your spiritual flab as you work on the ol' bod.

Discipline is the name of the game in keeping fit spiritually as well. You and I both know that if we simply make vague promises to "do better" with our daily spiritual disciplines like prayer and Bible reading, we won't. It's just too easy to get caught up in the bustle and confusion of everyday life and lose sight of our vision and goals.

We end up taking care of everyone but ourselves.

Sure, it's great when we vow to make changes on both spiritual and physical planes: to read our Bibles every day, "pray without ceasing" (1 Thessalonians 5:17 NKJV), make healthier eating choices, and limit

our food intake. But if we don't make a plan and then diligently work that plan, it just won't happen. We'll be like my friend Vickie whose off-the-cuff mantra is, "Just put me on a treadmill and feed me."

Nope, we definitely need discipline.

You don't simply wish for dinner and then sit back and wait for it to magically appear, do you? Well, come to think of it, I do. . .but *you* shouldn't. You plan your menu, do the shopping, prepare the food, and then pop it in the oven. Otherwise you'd end up with a growling tummy and an empty plate.

It's the same with both spiritual and physical fitness. No one ever said discipline is easy, but the end results (spiritual muscles of steel and a tight tush instead of cauliflower buns) are absolutely worth it.

> *Exercise is a dirty word. Every time I hear it,*
> *I wash my mouth out with chocolate.*
> Unknown

Taming the Beast

1. Do you feel that you're in control of your health? Why or why not?

2. Let's start small and work up from there. Pinpoint two fitness tips—one physical, one spiritual—you feel led to focus on for the next month. What steps can you take *today* to begin this fitness journey?

3. Read Ecclesiastes 4:9–10. If you're like me and discipline isn't your strong suit, consider enlisting a BFF to help you stay accountable in achieving your fitness goals. Believe me, a kindred spirit is an invaluable motivator for getting fit and staying fit.

Chapter 3
Waisting Away
(Body Awareness)

"Everything that lives and moves about will be food for you.
Just as I gave you the green plants, I now give you everything."

GENESIS 9:3 NIV

Okay, so you already know the year of my fiftieth birthday was my Debbie do-over year. Besides donning "invisible" braces to harness my protruding unicorn tooth, I decided to stop talking about losing weight and shut my mouth long enough to actually do it.

But I got less than I bargained for.

After dropping forty pounds, my heaping C cups turned into scant teaspoons. Freddie and Flopsie, who faithfully hung around for decades as my Bobbing Twins, were reduced to identical ant bites. My front looked a lot like my back—you couldn't tell if I was coming or going. I felt like a giant Gumby. I'd never worn padded bras in my life, but suddenly I had to buy contraptions rigged like cereal bowls lined with Kotex.

Why is it that in the battle of the bulge, unwanted baggage like flesh fanny packs, hip saddlebags, and thigh cellulite pouches fight to the bitter end, but our few assets are the first evacuees?

But I'm not complaining. A friend in her fifties who lost eighty-five pounds commented about her deflated bosoms: "They always used to bounce into a room ahead of me; now they drag in behind like a cape."

Many strange things happened when I shrank from a tight size 14 to 2. When leashed, my miniature poodle started whipping me around like the last car in a roller coaster. I could no longer push a full grocery cart uphill. I had to open heavy doors like a scrimmaging football linebacker.

And finding a size that fit? Forget it. Are any of us truly small, medium, or large?

My lifelong friend Don is a connoisseur. Some people are dessert connoisseurs; others are wine connoisseurs. Don is a *word* connoisseur. I knew something was strange about him since the sixth grade when I caught him reading the dictionary for fun.

Anyway, one day Don casually dropped the word *misogyny* during a Facebook chat. Now mind you, I'm a professional writer and that one stumped me. When I pondered its meaning, Don replied, "It means contempt for females. As in, 'The person who came up with the sizing system for women's clothing was the ultimate misogynist.' "

Ya got that right, bro. One-size-fits-all beach cover-ups are the biggest joke of all. Do they really fit *anybody*? We'd be better off cutting a head hole in a parachute.

And why, pray tell, with the disappearance of the equivalent of a gallon of cottage cheese from my abdomen, was my belly button still shaped like a frowny face? I expected one of those Frederick's of Hollywood I-shaped belly buttons. Nay, not so. I got a perpetually sad navel shaped like an eyebrow.

People react differently when you lose weight. Some applaud. Others bring you mounds of cheesecake. A few avoid you. Without missing a beat, my mother shifted gears from a lifetime mantra of "Put down that fork!" to "Eat! Eat! You look like a month-old apple core!"

One kind, sympathetic soul concluded that I could no longer

afford food and pulled me aside to offer a twenty. I suppose a recession *is* a dandy time to lose weight. Humorist Martha Bolton suggests a "Financial Stress Diet: When you feel like a snack, simply thumb through your stack of bills instead. It beats every appetite suppressant on the market."

As your frame reframes itself, long submerged body parts surface. One day as Spouse graciously massaged my shoulders, he recoiled as if snakebitten when his fingers collided with my protruding collarbone. "What. . .what is *that*?" he asked, bug-eyed. "We've been married thirty years and there've never been bones there before."

And who knew that the thick fat pad that used to cover my coccyx (tailbone) was there for a reason? All of a sudden I couldn't relax in the bathtub without a folded towel to cush my tush. Or sit on my car seat without an air doughnut.

That first Christmas was a real eye-opener. Embarrassed by my baggy lady wardrobe, my family presented me with clothing-store gift certificates. But there was a catch! My chic sister and fashionable twentysomething daughter insisted on shopping with me, vowing never to let me out of sight for fear I'd resort to buying the octogenarian polyester that once filled my closet.

I had previously resigned myself to elastic waists, over-blouses, and matronly styles since I could never seem to find anything cute in larger sizes. You know you're in trouble when you covet your eighty-four-year-old mother-in-law's outfit.

"Time to start over. You're updating," I was informed by my self-appointed wardrobe consultants. "All purchases must be approved by the fashion police." To my surprise, I actually liked some of the perky little numbers they piled into my dressing room. At least the ones not cut down to my frowning navel (since the Twins are no longer bobbing, cleavage is now what I do to a roast with a butcher knife).

Yet another glitch emerged.

My weight loss occurred during the winter while I was swathed in sweaters. So when spring sprang, I didn't recognize the pruney alien appendages extending from my armpits. Without sufficient meat to fill out their casings, my plump arms had shriveled like overgrilled sausages. And Dumbo ears had spouted out their backsides! Sagging skin flaps undulated and rippled where triceps used to be. It made me seasick to watch them in a mirror. My daughter laughed herself silly the first time I reached into the cupboard and my jumbo Dumbos whacked me upside the head. I could imagine my ER diagnosis: flab-induced concussion.

And I discovered why the *mature* Hollywood starlets wear turtlenecks. Without enough chub to support them, my naturally inherited turkey-wattle jowls suddenly descended into rivulets of wrinkles cascading down my neck. Instead of concealing the torrent, a top button merely dammed the flow. The loose skin pooled like congealed gravy and overflowed my collar.

I tried folding the skin wad neatly and tucking it into my collar, but every time I turned my head, the wattle escaped. I even considered alligator clips behind the ears.

During my Debbie do-over year, I discovered a fresh dependency on God for self-control, that elusive fruit of the Spirit that seems to be perpetually out of season. This dependency, in turn, led me to a new level of confidence that "I *can* do all things through Christ who strengthens me" (Philippians 4:13 NKJV, emphasis added).

I also found that by resolving some of my physical sources of acute self-consciousness, I was able to take my eyes off myself and focus more fully on spiritual growth. As my relationship with God strengthened, amazingly, so did my body image.

Now I'm rarely cognizant of my physical appearance (for better or for worse), and a lion's share of everyday stress has been relieved.

Sure, I lost a few inches, but you know what I found? Our outsides are not always reflections of our insides. You can look great but feel wretched. Botoxed on the outside but crinkle-fried on the inside. It doesn't matter that your teeth are straight if your attitude is warped. There's no magical cure for discontentedness or lagging self-esteem. If God's peace isn't in your heart when you're heavy, it won't be there when you're thin, either.

After all, God loves Sumo wrestlers just as much as runway models!

The older you get, the tougher it is to lose weight, because by then your body, soul and your fat are really good friends.

UNKNOWN

Taming the Beast

1. What are your sources of acute self-consciousness? Are there any physical issues that take your attention away from personal spiritual growth?
2. Do you feel as though you need a do-over year? In what way— physically, spiritually, emotionally, or all of the above? What's stopping you?
3. Can you think of a feasible plan to shift your energies inward instead of outward?

CHAPTER 4

Bermuda (Shorts) Triangle

(Fashion)

*And I want women to get in there…in humility before God, not
primping before a mirror or chasing the latest fashions but doing
something beautiful for God and becoming beautiful doing it.*

1 TIMOTHY 2:9–10 MSG

Looking fashionable is like an unquenchable thirst. Especially if you're
five-foot-nothing with legs the length of kumquats.

Take shorts, for example. I went to eight different stores before
stumbling across a pair of shorts that didn't make me look like a
Bavarian yodeler. Bermuda shorts cut us munchkins in two and give
the impression that the south half of our pants leg is MIA. Capris fall
just above our ankles like the high-waters Mrs. Noah probably sported
during the flood. Short shorts are definitely out. Avalanches of love
pudding (cellulite) elicit peculiar retching sounds from passersby. And
at my age, the shock of all that exposed skin making contact with air-
conditioned metal chairs would send me into cardiac arrest.

Bicycle shorts? Please! Encasing my quivering thighs in spandex is
like wrapping a rubber band around a wad of bread dough. Everything
squirts out whichever end is loosest.

Underwear shopping can be oh so confusing, too. Somehow
panties have become the new Lexus in status standards. I was perfectly
happy with plain white cotton briefs until I started changing at the
gym. Seems everyone else wears something akin to dental floss slung

between the two sides of a garter stretched over their hips. Pardon the pun, but I felt left behind (although some of the behinds I beheld would be better left unbeholden)!

Okay, shameful as it is, I'll admit caving to peer pressure (and my daughter's mortified, "Oh Motherrr—you're housing again!" every time she caught sight of my skivvies peeking above my belt). I compromised with lacy low-risers but saved my comfy grannies for my flannel nightie.

And bras—talk about making mountains out of molehills! Did you know that the first brassieres in America replaced rigid, full-body-length corsets at the beginning of the twentieth century when a New York socialite brazenly fashioned her own from ribbon and two handkerchiefs? The idea caught on and the bra evolved into a multimillion-dollar product. Cup sizes were introduced in 1922. Since that time, women have flirted with bras that are pointed, strapless, plunging, beefed up with cotton, water, or gel, and even unzipped for nursing.

Amazing the trivia you pick up at the lingerie counter.

One of my personal bra challenges has always been what to do with the Bobbing Twins while I play tennis. It seems the sports bra was invented in 1977 by a clever female runner who cut apart two athletic supporters and sewed them into the desired shape. Early sports bras did indeed curb concussions for large-busted gals, but they also squashed your breasts flat as an inverted mammogram.

I wore those steroidal training bras for a decade until Freddie and Flopsie evacuated when I lost weight. With little left to squash, I was delighted to discover pre-molded T-back sports bras that made the Twins look erect as little soldiers, although in reality, they bounced around the nearly empty cups like dice in a can. I appeared young and

perky zipping around the tennis court, albeit 95 percent faux. If you can't play like Venus, at least you can look out of this world, right?

Another of my fashion conundrums is accessories. Have you ever noticed that purse loyalties divide womandom like politics divide our nation? Such devotion toward swatches of leather and fabric!

You've got your two basic purse parties: bullmastiff (massive and intimidating) and Maltese (petite and adorable), with various trendy independent parties toting contraptions like moving vans with straps, Tic-Tac-sized micro-clutches, and glorified horse feed bags. Of course, there are sporadic bipartisan crossover occasions like beach trips or formal dinners when party lines blur, but in general, each purse party feels absolutely certain that its platform is superior and will fight to the death to defend it.

Fashion is an area of life where we can expect the unexpected. Like the time I swept into work at the rehab center, adorned in my new black pants. I admit I might have started styling a bit when I noticed a few patients staring at my chic outfit as I put my rottweiler purse away (can you tell which party I gravitate toward?). Then I heard a horrified gasp, and the secretary grabbed my arm.

"Debbie, *what* is on your rear end?" she whispered hoarsely.

"Uh, I don't know," I replied, turning circles like a mutt chasing his tail, unable to catch a glimpse of my dry-clean-only derriere. "Is it cat hair? My cat snuck into my car last night and was sleeping in the driver's seat when I went out to get the newspaper this morning."

"Nooo." She looked a little seasick. "It's definitely *not* hair. Chunks of something gooey and disgusting are stuck to your backside and dripping down your legs."

I loped into the bathroom to get a better view in the mirror. Apparently my ornery calico had upchucked her freshly digested

breakfast all over my driver's seat before I unknowingly wallowed in it. As I stood in my Fruit-of-the-Looms, scrubbing my nasty pants in the clinic sink while the secretary flitted about trying to help, I was glad at least my underwear was fashionable. The only thing worse than wearing regurgitated Friskies to work is high-top grannies.

Yes, sometimes it's hard to remember that nurturing a gentle and quiet spirit is more important than "chasing the latest fashions," as the apostle Paul warns in the passage at the beginning of this chapter. We fashion-chasers tend to buy in to the image-is-everything propaganda our culture feeds us, and have somehow intertwined physical appearance with affirmation of self-worth.

As if our personal value depends on how well we accessorize.

Paul was absolutely right when he said the way we *really* become beautiful is by doing something beautiful for God. Regardless of our appearance—how well we decorate this earth suit we've been assigned for a short time—true beauty answers to a higher, more exalted standard than bangle bracelets or tulle overlays.

No one will ever be more beautiful than Mother Teresa. Or Corrie ten Boom. Or Nellie Poss Rogers (my grandmother). Women who never wore diamond necklaces or silk camisoles or strappy heels in their lives, but radiated ethereal beauty the accessories of this world can't possibly mimic.

So the next time I'm trying on shorts, instead of succumbing to hopeless despair, I plan to dwell on the beautiful things I'm doing for God and let the cellulite fall where it may.

Fashion Law: If the shoe fits, it's ugly.

UNKNOWN

Taming the Beast

1. What's your biggest fashion challenge?
2. Which women do you consider truly beautiful, regardless of their appearance?
3. Can you name three beautiful things you're currently doing for God that make you beautiful, too?

CHAPTER 5

Not Just Plain Vanilla

(Behavior)

The fear of human opinion disables;
trusting in God protects you from that.

PROVERBS 29:25 MSG

The strange beating sound woke me around 2 a.m. I rolled out of my cozy bed, and with a quick glance at my sleep-through-a-hurricane husband, trudged in a sleepy stupor toward the direction of the unidentifiable racket.

In a dream-like trance, I unlocked my front door and stumbled down the walkway, where my attention was instantly drawn upward to the gigantic dragonfly hovering over my house. When the enormous insect caught sight of my slack-jawed self, it whirled in my direction, plastering my flimsy summer cotton nightie to my body with wind gusts strong enough to blow two rollers right out of my hair.

This dream was rapidly morphing into a Stephen King nightmare.

Only when the roaring dragonfly pinned me to the wall, with its blinding spotlight eyes, and its no-nonsense bullhorn voice instructed me to put my hands in the air did I finally awaken enough to realize I was confronting a police chopper and this was as real as it gets.

We've all heard from law enforcement officers that when it comes to criminals, you truly can't judge a book by its cover, that *everyone* is a suspect. The best disguise is to look "normal," to blend in like just another Hershey's Kiss in the candy dish. But I must admit that at that moment, I wanted to holler, "Okay, guys, how many people actually commit crimes barefoot in their jammies and curlers?"

I really was glad our deputies in blue were diligently pursuing the gas station robber who'd taken an escape route through my neighborhood, but it was a bit discombobulating to think that I might actually be a suspect. In the end, I was let off the hook, but it did make me wonder: Would someone ever be able to pick me out of a lineup? Or am I just a plain vanilla woman? Not tall, not short, not slim, not obese; a little wrinkly and saggy maybe, but not really distinctive in any way—just another fluffy, white sheep blending in with the rest of the mundane flock?

Humph. Didn't like that feeling one bit. I like to think I'm way past plain vanilla. I'm at least nutty fudge ripple.

Yet I was astonished to notice at my thirty-fifth high school reunion that about 90 percent of the women in the room were blonds. Now, very few of us were blonds back in the day, so it was tricky recognizing old gal pals as I swam upstream through the river of golden highlights. Apparently we had all hit upon the age-defying trick of camouflaging our burgeoning gray, but the joke was on us! We weren't fooling anyone—we were all the same age!

Still sheep after all those years, no ewe was willing to break out of the flock. We looked like a freeze-dried Norwegian ski team.

Several years ago, Constance Rhodes, a recovered bulimic and cofounder of the True Campaign, conducted an experiment in which she banned makeup for four weeks. Her goal was to confront her culturally inflicted beauty addiction head-on.

What did Constance learn by stripping away her mask, her cushion of self-protection, and bravely making herself vulnerable? Here's her wise conclusion: "Ultimately it's not whether or not I wear makeup that God cares about, but whether or not I'm in bondage to it."

You see, the makeup itself is not a problem; God wants us to present ourselves as the best we can be.

The real issue is our dependency upon augmentation of our God-given appearance for acceptance and self-esteem, whether through makeup, surgical alterations, or high fashion. How dependent are we on external fixes to feel that we fit in? Are accepted? Are attractive? He created us, each and every one a masterpiece—in our natural state, rough-hewn and raw. And He loves us lavishly, just that way.

Not one of us is plain vanilla! Our flavor comes through the creative passion of our Master Designer, not how we decorate ourselves.

Okay, I know sometimes it's easier to think, *She got the job instead of me because she looks like a supermodel and I look like a Chevy model*, or *That good-looking guy's ignoring me because my hair looks like fresh roadkill*, rather than deal with personal flaws we really need to address or wrestle through deeper rejection issues.

Let's face it: appearance *can* make a difference in how others treat us. But that doesn't mean we have to *feel* flawed and rejected. Not at all!

Old Testament Esther was a woman whose station in life was totally based on appearance. She really *did* get her job because she looked like a supermodel. And to remain queen (and even retain her head on her shoulders), she had to keep her lusty husband-king satiated with eye candy. Can you imagine the pressure of looking drop-dead gorgeous every moment of every day?

But Esther didn't allow the trappings of beauty to hold her captive. She learned to *use* beauty—while not abusing it—to accomplish God's purposes. Grab your Bible and let's look at a few transcendent points from Esther's story, which we can apply to our own lives today:

- Purity is important (see Esther 2:2). Esther, although considered one of the most beautiful women in the kingdom, was a virgin. This was no accident. She valued her chastity and took virtue seriously. She saved herself for the right man at the right time in God's eyes.

- Background doesn't matter (see Esther 2:5–7). Esther was an orphaned descendant of slaves. God doesn't need pedigreed people to accomplish His purposes. "He raises the poor from the dust. . .he seats them with princes and has them inherit a throne of honor" (1 Samuel 2:8 NIV).

- Be more than just a pretty face (see Esther 2:12–15). Although Esther endured twelve months of mandatory beauty treatments before her audition with the king, scores of other women were equally lovely. Esther didn't depend on her own assets, but humbly followed the advice of those wiser than she to shine above all others. She was only one of many diamonds glittering in the jewelry case, but Esther's wisdom and virtue sparkled brightest.

- We live "for such a time as this" (Esther 4:14 NIV). All the days of our lives are preparation for a specific work God intends for us, that incredible, fulfilling moment when His glory is revealed in us. Esther was made queen for one purpose: to save her people. Sister, what is your purpose?

- Seek prayer and support from others (see Esther 4:15–16). She knew she couldn't do it alone, so Esther asked her cousin to have all the Jews in the city pray for her to have the courage to lay her life on the line, approach the king, and expose the liar threatening her people.

- Courage means doing it afraid (see Esther 4:15–16). We may not be brave before our trial, but God will enable us to take that crucial step when we need it most. He specializes in holding our quivering, sweaty hands and walking *with* us through our worst fears.

- Trust is believing there's *always* a tomorrow, that if you follow God's plan, everything's gonna be all right. The worst that can happen is that you close your eyes on earth and wake up in heaven. "I'll go to the king, even though it's forbidden. If I die, I die" (Esther 4:16 MSG).

- Brains are never overrated (see Esther 5:1–5). Our girl hatched a clever plan, using all the tools available to her. Femininity and craftiness are gifts from God, tied with a lace bow. Whether we open them or not is up to us.

- Our downtimes are God's working-behind-the-scenes times (see Esther 5:7–8). Esther obeyed the risky idea God put in her head to *wait*, to be patient, to request a second banquet in which to spill the beans. This ploy not only enticed and beguiled the king, but it paved the way for Esther's ultimate victory. The extra waiting time not only made Esther's enemy, Haman, work up a frothy furor and build the gallows that eventually became his own demise, but made the king's sleepless night, during which he wondered what Esther was up to, result in even more humiliation for Haman (see Esther 6 and 7).

- Patience allows the stew to thicken (see Esther 7:1–6). Esther waited until her man was fed, wined, and feeling frisky before springing her news. Full tummies pave the way for gratitude and generosity.

- Gossip can ruin everything (see Esther 7:3–6). Esther wisely said nothing behind her enemy's back until she was ready to say it to his face.
- We find "light and gladness and joy and honor" (Esther 8:16 NASB) only in the center of God's will. Nowhere else. *Nowhere else.*

Don't you just *love* that girl? Esther wasn't afraid to break away from the flock. She trusted God to protect her from the fear of others' opinions. I want to be like that. Not just another sheep. Not plain ol' vanilla. Unique in Jesus' name.

So the next time I'm pinned to the wall by a monstrous one-eyed dragonfly and end up in a police lineup, all fingers will point to the unmistakable triple-mocha-mint-chocolate-chip-crunch girl. *Moi!*

> *Always be a first-rate version of yourself instead of a second-rate version of somebody else.*
> JUDY GARLAND

Taming the Beast

1. So, girl, what flavor are you? What flavor do you want to be?
2. What are your unique qualities? Could someone pick you out of a lineup?
3. Which part of Esther's story resonates most with you? For me, it's striving to find what living for "such a time as this" means for my life. How about you?

CHAPTER 6
Hot to Go

(Maturing Gratefully)

"He will renew your life and sustain you in your old age."

RUTH 4:15 NIV

Contrary to the belief of ill-informed youth, while other body systems are declining as women age, there is one system on *GO*: appreciation of a fine male physique. I learned this unexpectedly, of all places, in front of 150 kids in children's church.

As I took the stage and began teaching a lesson about becoming a "Commando for Christ," Jonas, a volunteer dad fifteen years my junior, jogged onstage in his form-fitting white T-shirt and army fatigues.

Whoa, mama! Caught off guard by my fiftysomething hormones being jolted from hibernation, my eyes bulged and a sharp intake of breath sucked my mouth dry.

Jonas had been fully clothed when we ran through the sketch backstage. In his tight undershirt, he was a lot more, um, *well defined.* I was suddenly brain-dead as he barked out his rehearsed line in military fashion: "I'm here to report for duty as one of the Ten Commandos, ma'am."

Blindsided by the rippling muscles in Jonas's Schwarzenegger-in-the-'80s physique, I lost my grip. On my composure and on the microphone. *Bam.* It hit the wooden floor and rolled across the stage to the accompaniment of a horrendous squeal. The children grabbed their ears. Diving for the elusive mic, I fumbled around on my hands

and knees as Jonas patiently continued to jog in place.

Finally, red-faced and panting, I retrieved it (the mic, not my dignity). What in the world was going on with me? What in the world was my next line?

I could only stand dumbstruck, gawking at those bulging biceps and perfect pecs. Jonas was the one running; why was I breaking into a sweat? Backstage, several women snickered behind their hands, clueing me in that I was sooo busted!

Jonas, unaware of what was going down, repeated his line. Louder. As if I were hard of hearing, for pity's sake.

"I'm here to report for duty as one of the Ten Commandos, ma'am."

Realizing I had to say *something*, I cleared my throat and uttered the only lucid thought in my head: "And a fine specimen you are, too, soldier."

I am forever grateful that the angel-commandos in God's celestial army didn't, at that moment, smite me upside the head with their flaming swords.

Reckon my mutinying hormones haven't completely jumped ship. Spouse will be glad to hear that. That is, if he's tuned in to my frequency when I tell him. We've been married over thirty years and have perfected the fine art of selective hearing. His receiver doesn't always pick up my broadcasted waves and vice versa, so we sometimes accuse each other of faulty amplifiers when it's actually a tower problem.

Despite the occasional power outage, our love actually blazes stronger and deeper than ever after three decades of marital blitz. I mean bliss. Anyway, I've grown to appreciate the sentiment of Agatha Christie, the famous murder-mystery author: "An archaeologist is the best husband a woman can have; the older she gets, the more interested

he is in her."

The good news is that middle age has its benefits. I make lots of new friends. I frequently meet people for the first time whom I've met before.

Perfection takes time. Hey, oak trees don't produce their best acorns until they've lived half a century! I bowled the best game of my life at age fifty-one. My bad self rolled a 183 using an eight-pound ball *without bumper rails*! (I could have done even better if the silly ball hadn't kept bouncing off pins without even making them wobble.)

Aging is good. For cheese. And the best meats marinate for a looong time (ever been compared to a rump roast?).

Speaking of long waits, some cicadas finally emerge to maturity after a decade-long underground gestation. By the way, did you know cicadas are one of the rare insects that actually *sweat*? How about that? A bug that's perpetually late, is obnoxiously loud, constantly repeats itself, and has hot flashes. Our teensy-weensy menopausal mascot!

Maturity should be our most productive season of life. I don't know about you, but I refuse to die before my actual death. I asked God for more hours in the day to get everything done and He sent me menopause. Now I have the nighttime, too!

Yep, after many years of trial and error, we finally have a grip on our unique set of gifts and abilities, and we can gratefully determine how best to use them for God's glory. Of course, memory may not serve to recall those abilities an hour from now. If you're like me, your photographic memory hasn't been fully developed. Thoughts hop around my mind like a moth on a lightbulb and most of them sizzle into dust before they can embed themselves in my brain.

Our eyesight might be on the fritz, but our insight is keener than ever. We've learned to take our eyes off the mirror and focus on things

more important—things of eternal value, such as taking as many of our loved ones to heaven with us as we can—not at the same time, of course.

As we cross that invisible half-century line, we can't deny that a few physical changes do take place. Like varicose veins that pop and sizzle like tiny zags of electricity. Harry Potter has nothing on me—he may have a lightning bolt on his forehead but I have fifty on my left leg alone.

Or those previously plump, robust earlobes drooping to our Crocs after decades of decorating ourselves with heavy earring baubles. Ever notice how in young folks, the piercing hole is a tiny dot? As we age, that dot elongates into a long wobbly slash. I tell people Captain Jack Sparrow ran his sword through my piercing hole in a fit of passion.

Honey, don't I wish!

Did you know there are actually laser earlobe treatments and a medical procedure called "earlobe rejuvenation" where fillers are injected to remove wrinkles, making those dangling skin flaps appear "fuller and more youthful." Ha! Just what we need to draw even more attention to ourselves—adolescent earlobes attached to a tree-bark face. Talk about pouring new wine into old wineskins! "No one pours new wine into old wineskins. Otherwise, the new wine will burst the skins. . .and the wineskins will be ruined" (Luke 5:37 NIV).

Then there is the Clark Gable phenomenon that appears on the upper lip when estrogen disappears. At least some of us don't have to worry about the spiderweb lines around our lips—the mustache covers them right up. And what's with those pesky stray chin hairs that sprout like weeds in a petunia patch?

Cleavage suddenly quits cleaving and we find that the best reason to wear low-cut shirts is to funnel crumbs down to our belly buttons to

collect for a snack later.

We mustn't overlook the PAH: physiological aging hypothesis (one of my newest Coty near-facts of science). PAH states that as a woman's age creeps northward, her body parts travel south, and hips expand to incredible new horizons east to west. Hey, we hot mamas are all over the map!

According to Bob Hope, middle age is when our age starts to show around the middle. But our middle years are when we can finally discover and fulfill our deeper purpose. Not just reflect on what we could or should do, but actually *do* it. That's right, spring into action! Sometimes the difference between action and good intentions is trust and obey versus rust and decay.

You heard me, girl—spring into action! Forget the previous abilities that refuse to cooperate and prime new skills until they're hot to go. It's time to kick your own *but*—*but* I can't because. . .*but* I never have before. . .*but* what if I fail?. . .*but, but, but*.

But nothin'! Let's lose the excuses and get off our *buts*. Memory loss may not be such a bad thing. We can do amazing things if we forget that we can't!

It's sad to grow old, but nice to ripen.
BRIGITTE BARDOT

Taming the Beast

1. You may not identify with my fiftysomething body changes yet (or maybe you've been there, done that), but what physical changes are you currently dealing with?
2. Which new skills are you priming as we speak?
3. Are you ready to join me in getting off our *buts*?

Chapter 7
Show Dog with Fleas

(Image)

What matters is not your outer appearance—
the styling of your hair, the jewelry you wear,
the cut of your clothes—but your inner disposition.

1 Peter 3:3–4 msg

I was surprised to see the title winner, the champion, the top dog—in real life. For dog shows, he was groomed to a luster, head high and nails buffed, but without the crowd, stage, and judges, he looked like any other scruffy mutt scratching his fleas. He was a regular dirt muffin.

It got me thinking about how we sometimes live double lives, too. The image we project isn't who we truly are. All glitter, grace, and effervescent smiles in public, but turn us loose behind closed doors and watch us growl and snarl and bite.

Then the pumpkin incident drove the point home.

Last October, I decorated a pumpkin to match a picture I saw in *Good Housekeeping*. My "harvest pumpkin" was a sight to behold, with lovely silk ribbon pinned in stripes up the sides and gathered on top with a burst of fall flowers. Exquisite, everyone said. A real showpiece.

Fall came and went, then Christmas, and my harvest pumpkin looked just as pretty as ever. So I continued proudly displaying it month after month through winter and spring.

In late April, I arrived home from a week's vacation to find my harvest pumpkin had collapsed into a sticky, smelly orange puddle on the floor. Although once gorgeous on the outside, it had rotted on the inside, finally imploding into a disgusting mess.

Hmm. Could I, like the Harvest Pumpkin, have a facade? Am I different in private than in public?

If I'm serious about emulating Christ, there shouldn't be a difference between my inward and outward image. My Christian persona should be the real deal, not just for show. My insides should be as fresh, beautiful, and orange as my outsides. Well, maybe not orange.

It's an uncomfortable subject for most Christians—this double-life conundrum. We don't like to admit that yes, well, maybe sometimes we do tend to put on the dog. The show dog. To yell at our families at home and then appear at church like Laura Bush on Xanax. To cheat on our taxes while teaching in Sunday school that stealing is wrong. To proclaim to our kids that Jesus wants us to love our neighbor as ourselves and then scream hair-curling jerk-scenities behind the steering wheel.

Jesus confronted the vileness of hypocrisy in Matthew 23:13–39. He lamented, "Woe to you" no less than seven times in this single chapter and associated being a show dog with the terms, "blind guides," "snakes," and "brood of vipers" (NIV).

Strong words. Make no mistake: The Almighty has strong feelings about this subject.

So where is our disconnect? Could it be that we live double lives because we're simply unwilling to surrender all facets of ourselves to God? To hand over all our masks? Maybe it's a pride issue. We want to decide which mask we'll wear and for whom. Concealing our true selves becomes our secret shame and we end up as show dogs. With fleas.

Image can be a double-edged sword. Sometimes we unknowingly project someone we're not, and sometimes we intentionally don a guise for all the wrong reasons. Maybe we don't like who we really are. Or we yearn to appear smarter, more successful, or sexier.

A thirtysomething newly divorced woman with a preteen son moved to my town and began mowing the yard while wearing her bikini. It was mind-boggling how her lawn care day suddenly became the yard work day of choice for the he-neighbors. She wore shorty-shorts (remember when we used to call them "hot pants"?) and halter tops to the grocery and bank, and tight, low-cut blouses to work. I have to admit that I judged her by appearance only and couldn't have been more shocked to learn she was a Christian.

When I got past her fast-lane veneer and the loose-woman reputation I had ungraciously pinned on her, I found a wounded, insecure sister who was terrified of being alone. She desperately wanted to find a father for her troubled son and was trying to attract men the only way she knew how.

In our zeal to attain beauty, we have to remember that it's fine to look modern, even chic, but not at the sacrifice of integrity. "GOD can't stand deceivers, but oh how he relishes integrity" (Proverbs 11:20 MSG).

Modesty is never outdated to the Lord.

It's probably fair to say that we all tweak our image at one time or another—straightening seams and spit-slicking every hair into place before that meeting with the boss to portray the model of efficiency; donning a creamy silk blouse for a romantic evening out with the little mister; cramming a size 12 booty into size 8 jeans for the high school reunion picnic.

Sister, there's not a thing wrong with presenting the best "you" possible. God is pleased when we respect His handiwork enough to put our prettiest toenails forward.

The problem arises when we become consumed with manipulating our image in order to control what other people think of us. *Control* is the key word here. We're really fighting the Lord for control when we're obsessing about how we appear to others. It becomes all about impressing other weak humans like us, not proudly expressing the brushstrokes of the masterpiece that Papa God purposefully created in us.

The mirror of our lives should reflect Jesus, not the Marilyn Monroe we wish we were.

One afternoon my daughter dropped by just as I arrived home from a speaking event. Her eyes popped out of her head as she gasped, "Motherrr, please tell me you didn't stand in front of a room full of women in *that* getup!" (I'm usually *Mom* except when she's appalled at something I've done, which, come to think of it, is most of the time.) This was after I started losing weight and before my shopping spree with the fashion police.

I rotated before the foyer full-length mirror (oops—should have done that before I left!) to find that my short cardigan didn't begin to hide the jumbo diaper pin holding up my pants in back, fully exposing the overlapped fabric that came to two crisp points over my bum. I looked like the 1980s cone-bra Madonna, upside down and backward.

You know what, girlfriend? We don't need an image manager. . . we need an image in a manger. If we focus on the Christ Child who was born dirt-poor in a lowly stable—not in an opulent palace *by His design*—only to grow to manhood in the most modest of circumstances and then die penniless on a criminal's cross for our sins, we can't help but remain humble. Only with our eyes on Him are our true selves revealed.

We all struggle to keep our eyes on the Creator and not on the created (ourselves). I actually cringed when a man in my couples Bible study group commented, "My, Debbie, you look very wholesome tonight."

Wholesome? That was *not* the look I was going for. Attractive, lovely, feminine, ravishing—even color-coordinated would have been welcomed. But *wholesome*? Isn't cracked wheat wholesome?

Then the more I thought about it, I realized that was actually one of the nicest compliments I've ever received. Wholesome is precisely the way Papa God desires for me to be perceived, especially by men who aren't my husband. "God doesn't require attention-getting devices" (Matthew 6:18 MSG).

The apostle Paul correlates wholesomeness with the "edification" of others in Ephesians 4:29 (NASB). The definition of *edification* is "improvement in morality." So what Paul is saying is that we should present ourselves to others in a way that improves them—builds up their character—not only by our appearance, but in our speech and actions as well.

That means no pretenses, false fronts, or role-playing to build ourselves up in the eyes of others. Why? Because our focus is on *them,* not us.

Wow—what a relief! It's way too hard to keep up the show-dog facade, isn't it? Downright draining. How much easier to be one person. . .inside and out. . .to any audience. . .at all times.

And we won't even have to worry about finding rhinestone flea collars!

Beauty is not caused. It is.

EMILY DICKINSON

Taming the Beast

1. Do you feel that your public image leans toward show dog? Are you the same in public as you are in private?
2. Don't feel embarrassed if you wear masks; most of us do. The thing is, are you trying to look like Jesus or someone else?
3. Think a minute about your appearance. Is your focus on building up others? If not, what changes might you make to shift your focus to where it should be?

CHAPTER 8

Hanging Up the Invisibility Cloak

(Building Confidence)

*She answered God by name, praying to the God who spoke to her,
"You're the God who sees me! Yes! He saw me; and then I saw him!"*

GENESIS 16:13 MSG

There I was, supine in the gynecologist's office again, chilled and vulnerable in the humiliating *position*—you know the one—waiting for the doctor to swoop in and do his thing. I snickered over the comic some enterprising soul had tacked on the ceiling above the examining table. The strip depicted a clueless husband leaving his wife a note on the fridge door, reading, "Honey, the doctor called and your Pabst beer is normal. So when did you start drinking?"

Finally two young female medical assistants breezed in, chattering to each other as if I weren't even there. Their conversation never broke stride as one whipped my paper gown out from the full-coverage cocoon I had painstakingly fashioned around me and pried my clenched knees apart.

Precisely why I've always thought GYN stands for "groping your nether-regions."

Then the medical assistant's eyes locked on something way down yonder beneath the canopy of my paper tent. Her face took on a "Eww!" expression as she exclaimed to her coworker, "Oh my gosh— what in the world is *that*?"

"What is *what*?" I asked, feeling dread rise in my innards like a five-alarm fire. What could possibly be abnormal enough about my privates to elicit such a reaction?

"Oh—that's too bad," the other barely-out-of-her-teens gal agreed. "That's gotta be one of the worst ones I've ever seen."

"Yeah," the first girl said. "She's not all that old, either."

Hey! I'm right here! I may be old enough to be your grandm—Well, maybe your aunt—but I'm not dead yet! I wanted to yell. *What's wrong down there? Talk to me!*

Before I could spit a single frenzied thought out of my mouth, the first cheerleader-in-scrubs tapped the twelve-inch scar zigzagging down my left leg and casually remarked, "That really is a nasty piece of work. Wonder how she did it?"

Aargh!

Do you, too, ever feel invisible? Like life is swirling all around you but you aren't included? Like people look right through you as if you're not worth focusing on?

When we feel invisible, we often pretend it doesn't matter for the sake of self-preservation. That's how we keep our sanity and don't run screaming into the night. But it *does* matter. It matters to us and it matters to God, who created us for significance.

"How precious are your thoughts about me, O God. They cannot be numbered! I can't even count them; they outnumber the grains of sand!" (Psalm 139:17–18 NLT).

Invisibility is like a thick blanket that smothers our potential. It can become a good excuse to not try. When we operate under the assumption that no one notices us, the pressure's off to try to improve ourselves, to become more spiritually beautiful, to grow in our representation of Christ. Our insecurity expands unchecked and unheeded, and eventually we quit caring.

Sometimes we find comfort in invisibility and actually welcome it. We try to blend in, fly under the radar, lie low. Like at the grocery store when you run inside for just two items and hope against hope that nobody recognizes you in your stained sweatshirt, Chia Pet hairdo, and naked face.

But then there are other times when we yearn to be noticed, when our greatest desire is to be of consequence to someone. To be respected. To be accepted.

Don't you just love the scripture at the beginning of this chapter, when Hagar—the mistreated, runaway, second-banana servant-wife of Abraham—suddenly realizes that she's *not* invisible? That God actually sees her? That she matters to Him when she doesn't feel like she matters to anyone else on the face of the earth?

Have you ever felt that way? Forgotten by all mankind and totally amazed that the Creator of the universe cares personally about *you*? I know I have. Maybe it's because of the inaccurate way we view ourselves.

We look into a mirror and see an image, but not the same image God sees. Our vision, our self-perception, has been jaded by labels we've received our entire lives. We still wear labels that were callously glued onto our backs from childhood, stamps like *klutzy*, *stupid*, *not good enough*, or *fatty-fatty-two-by-four, can't fit through the bathroom door* (my personal nemesis). And then there are other labels we've assigned ourselves as we've grown up, like *airhead*, *idiot*, *loser*, or *damaged goods*.

These types of labels erode our confidence and work subtly, beneath the surface, to make us feel worthless. The internal damage is often reflected externally in our posture or countenance. We may slump our shoulders, hang our heads, keep our eyes downcast, or throw our hands in the air and give up on our appearance altogether. Why bother?

We wear these destructive labels so long we eventually get used to

them and aren't even aware of their presence. Or power. Our thinking is shaped by them, which then subconsciously modifies our behavior to fit our label. It becomes a vicious cycle.

I often get frustrated when my daughter is trying to teach me some new technological gizmo that I can't seem to grasp. I find myself pulling out the *dumb* label I keep tucked inside my shirt (I know it's always there but others don't) and posting it clearly across my chest in neon letters. Wearing this label, I feel justified that I can't learn anything new; it's just who I am—"the way God made me."

But Cricket doesn't buy it. "Mom," she says in a hard, unsympathetic tone, "quit playing dumb; it won't work. I know you're not stupid. You're a college graduate, an author, and a medical professional. You *can* get this. Now stop hiding behind the 'old dog' mask and concentrate on this 'new trick.'"

What secret labels do you have tucked inside your shirt? Do you hide them so well that nobody knows they're there but you? I've got news for you, sister: Someone else knows and He ain't buying it, either.

Labels can build us up or tear us down. Some women wear a *chic* label proudly, or maybe *trendy*, *wealthy*, or *politically correct*. Others work hard to earn labels like *professional*, *successful*, *efficient*, *intelligent*, or *competent*. Still others become known by their beliefs as *pro-life*, *godly*, *activist*, or *conservative*.

We rely on labels to clarify our identity, don't we? If we're not sure who we really are—or maybe don't *like* who we really are—we can hide behind a designer label that reflects who we wish we were. Something classy, perhaps, to give us a feeling of importance.

As a fashion-conscious teenager, I carefully cut the Tommy label off a pair of worn-out, hand-me-down jeans and sewed it onto my Kmart specials. That pants-hopping label kept me in style for many years!

(Now don't roll your eyes—you've probably done the same thing!)

But you know what? God doesn't believe in labels. He doesn't even notice the stickers we've plastered all over ourselves. When we invite Jesus into our hearts and ask Him to fill us with His love, all God sees when He looks at us is the gentle, sweet, beautiful reflection of His Son.

So how do we become visible? How do we permanently shed that cloak of invisibility with all its hang-ups?

It's quite simple, but not at all easy. We must refuse to believe the pernicious labels. Rip them off and shred those suckers. Call them lies from the pit of hell—that's what they are. Resolve to no longer accept the false identity we've allowed ourselves to be branded with for more years than we can remember. Leave the comfort zone of who we *think* we are—it wasn't all that great anyway.

The first step is identifying the labels that define you. It may be helpful to engage the help of a trusted friend or family member for this part. Make a list of labels. Write them down. Check off the edifying labels and use a red marker to cross through the derogatory ones. These are the ones you're planning to delete from the hard drive of your being.

Now, the second step is the really crucial part: Every time one of those old poisonous labels pops out from under your shirt and sneaks a corrupting thought into your head, recognize it, delete it, and replace it with a positive label.

For example, when I was recently wrestling with a new computer program that seemed way over my head and my *dumb* label began to creep out of my collar, I recognized it, called it what it was ("You're nothing but an ugly lie from the great deceiver!"), and replaced it with positive labels redefining me as *motivated, achiever, hard-worker,* and *smarter than a fifth-grader.* I believe I *am* all those things; I just

wasn't fully conscious of it at that weak moment. . .until I intentionally focused on my productive labels instead of wallowing in the destructive one.

And the third step: *Act* visible—you're representing the Creator of all things! Stand up straight; pull the cord! "Pulling the cord" is a little trick I learned in therapy school to correct posture. Here's how it works: Pretend there's a cord attached to your sternum between your breasts. Pull the cord upward, which will elevate your rib cage and shift your body into proper alignment so there's a vertical line from your ear to your shoulder, hip, and knee.

Voilà! Now you look like the princess you are as a daughter of the King!

Above all, remember that when you ask Jesus to fill you with His presence, you have a new identity; a pure, healthy, holy, *confident* identity. The old labels are obsolete. It's like intentionally enrolling in the witness protection program—you get to begin anew in the richness of your identity in Christ. "Anyone who belongs to Christ is a new person. The past is forgotten, and everything is new" (2 Corinthians 5:17 CEV).

Now c'mon, girl, start afresh! It's a brand-new day. Pull that cord. Hold your head up. You're not faux Prada or Gucci or Ralph Lauren anymore; you're the unique, gorgeous *real* thing! Proudly wear the label of *the* Master Designer!

> *Beauty without grace is the hook without the bait.*
> RALPH WALDO EMERSON

Taming the Beast

1. Do you usually feel like everyone is watching you or no one at all? When was the last time you felt invisible?

2. Are there any unfair labels that have stuck to you since childhood? What secret labels do you keep tucked inside your shirt?

3. Are you visible in your new, confident identity as a Master Designer original? If not, maybe it's time to pull that cord and begin!

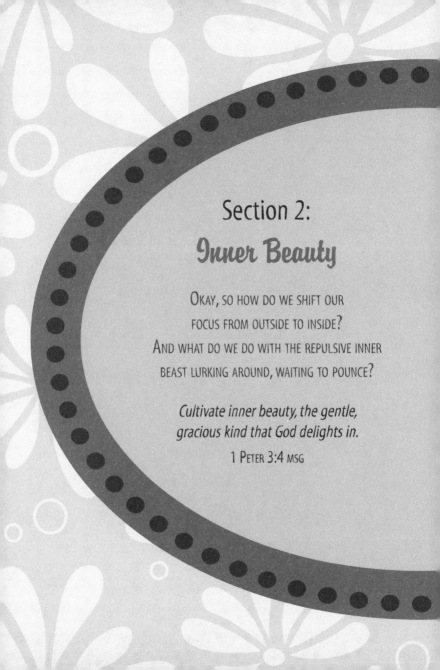

Section 2:
Inner Beauty

OKAY, SO HOW DO WE SHIFT OUR
FOCUS FROM OUTSIDE TO INSIDE?
AND WHAT DO WE DO WITH THE REPULSIVE INNER
BEAST LURKING AROUND, WAITING TO POUNCE?

*Cultivate inner beauty, the gentle,
gracious kind that God delights in.*
1 PETER 3:4 MSG

CHAPTER 9

Inside Out

(God's Beauty Standard)

*Don't become so well-adjusted to your culture that you fit
into it without even thinking. Instead, fix your attention on God.
You'll be changed from the inside out.*

ROMANS 12:2 MSG

My coworker Alexa, a hand therapist, was single, twentysomething, and the epitome of trendy. She wouldn't be caught dead in a blouse that wasn't Armani and always wore chic outfits with designer shoes to work, even though the other clinicians wore comfortable flats and scrubs.

One day, Alexa exited the ladies' room in a smidge too much of a hurry and wondered why the heads of patients, therapists, and physicians swiveled in her direction as she strode across the clinic. It was only when she reached her work station that she realized the back hem of her skirt was caught in the waistband of her panties, offering exclusive southern exposure.

Beauty can be such a beast.

You've got to respect Webster's definition of *beauty*: "Qualities that exalt the mind or spirit." That means our truly *beautiful* qualities—external or internal—serve to uplift, heighten, and enhance ourselves and others.

We all want to feel beautiful. But I have to admit that exalting the spirit is the furthest thing from my mind when I'm bathing suit shopping. I just want to keep my qualities from causing onlookers to upchuck their chicken nuggets. How much longer will I have to wait until bathing bloomers come back in style?

I find the judgment pronounced by those horrendous three-way dressing room mirrors worse than any judgment God would ever render. They have *no* mercy. *No* sympathy. You can't escape your flaws; they're exposed from every possible angle in the glare of unforgiving white light. It's like standing naked center stage on Broadway. Nowhere to hide. *Anything.*

And no matter how many bathing suits you try on, you keep thinking, *The next one's got to be better.* So you work your way through mountains of spandex and finally realize the only way you're going to find a suit that'll hold everything together is to cut one from the trampoline in your backyard.

Sigh. Solomon was right: "All is vanity" (Ecclesiastes 1:2 KJV).

The Bible reminds us that as thinking women, we should realize that external beauty is temporary and subjective and as fleeting as platform heels or big hair. Here today, gone by suppertime. That principle is easy enough to prove by the boxes of fur-trimmed miniskirts and plaid bell-bottoms we've excised from our closets.

God's values and the world's are just the opposite. It's our inside-out kind of beauty that's most important to Him—the only thing of eternal value. Even so, sometimes we all wrestle with keeping our attention focused on God and not on designer jeans. Especially if there's a sale at Macy's.

Real beauty can only come from God's inside-out love. When we finally comprehend His extravagant and intimate love for us, from our flat feet to our split ends, then our heart-glow will reflect radiant beauty from the inside out. We'll finally *feel* beautiful.

Only when we feel truly loved are we free to feel truly lovely.

It's really a good thing to make the most of our appearance; I believe God is pleased when our motivation is to be the best we can be to reflect the glory of our Creator. The problem arises when our motivation insipidly morphs into reflecting our own glory: the glory of the *created*. Then we risk becoming obsessive fashionistas. Coveting becomes a way of life. Jealousy flares. Greed flourishes. Stress escalates.

Our inside-out focus reverses to outside-in; we lose sight of our upward purpose and fall into a downward spiral.

But, sister, take heart! Striking a spiritually healthy balance *is* possible. It just takes conviction and effort—like anything worthwhile. Lassoing and corralling our rogue cravings are an important part of maturing spiritually. "We take captive every thought to make it obedient to Christ" (2 Corinthians 10:5 niv).

Taking those greedy thoughts captive doesn't happen in one fell swoop. It's more nurture than nature. . .a process. Much like the process used by the candy maker I observed in a quaint chocolate shoppe during a mountain vacation. The skilled craftswoman poured a fresh batch of boiling fudge onto a huge marble slab and quickly began using a specialized metal spatula to scoop up the cooling edges and fold the hardening chocolate back into the soft center mass. She patiently continued her vigil, circling round and round the slab, working the thickening fudge constantly until it was ready to mold into its finished form.

Our thoughts are like that unformed fudge. Left on their own, they'd spread out everywhere, oozing over the edges of God's parameters until they ended up a nasty, useless mess on the floor. But with a spatula of consistent guidance and discipline, we can scoop up our rogue thoughts and rework them into something valuable, beneficial, and delicious.

Well, maybe not delicious (I'm still drooling over that fudge). But you get my drift, right?

Just remember, it's a learning curve and we're bound to blow it occasionally. For instance, the impulse that forsakes all else to be first in line for that Gucci blowout sale is one of those temptations common to man (or to woman in this case). Paul addresses temptation in 1 Corinthians 10:13: "No temptation has overtaken you except what is common to mankind. And God is faithful; he will not let you be tempted beyond what you can bear. But when you are tempted, he will also provide a way out so that you can endure it" (NIV).

Yup. Temptation *seizes* us. Isn't that just the perfect word for it? Temptation seizes us in its vise-grip talons like a gigantic pterodactyl swooping in, plucking us out of our safe warm nests, and flying away with us.

Hey—I don't want to be temptation's lunch, do you? We don't have to helplessly succumb. We can fight back!

My foolproof way to escape a temptation attack is to keep prayer lists in my purse and car so that when those talons begin piercing my skin over that enticing dress or cute hat, I'm prepared. (Yes, I said *hat*— I'll admit I'm a hat girl; dozens bedeck every square inch of my closet walls.) I pull out my prayer list and turn my attention to the needs of others. My focus shifts off my petty desires and onto those for whom I desire to be Christ's hands and feet. The wicked pterodactyl releases me. Works every time!

Why don't you try it? Buy a couple of little 99-cent flip pads and stash them in handy places. Pull them out at red lights, in waiting rooms, while the kids have team practice, or any time you find a free moment. Keep a running prayer list and don't forget to record God's answers.

Fill your mind with prayer and your spirit will be exalted. That's true beauty shining from the inside out! In *Beauty by the Book,* author and TV celebrity Nancy Stafford puts it so well: "The best beauty advice isn't about the latest beauty products and has nothing to do with anything you buy or apply. It has to do with the inner radiance that comes from a tended-to spirit and joy-filled experiences."

So when that beauty beast tries to take a bite out of your hide, or impale you with his razor-sharp talons, be prepared. Kick him in the teeth (with your best pointy-toed boots) and send him yelping.

Beauty—in projection and perceiving—is 99.9 percent attitude.

GREY LIVINGSTON

Taming the Beast

1. Name three of your beautiful qualities that exalt the minds or spirits of your friends. Nope, one won't do. . .think of *three*. Now focus on those!
2. What runaway thoughts do you need to work on taking captive?
3. Do you keep a mobile prayer list? If not, why not start one today?

CHAPTER 10
Get Your Bad Self Down
(Taking a Spiritual Retreat)

After bidding them farewell,
He [Jesus] left for the mountain to pray.

MARK 6:46 NASB

Ever worry that if you looked in a spiritual mirror, you'd see the reflection of Snow White's ugly, snarling wicked witch dangling a juicy red apple from her clawed fingertips? The temptation to forego our daily God time is strong these days, yet the busier we are, the more we *need* the inner peace that only He can give.

I think we all reach a point in our lives when fifteen minutes of quiet time in the morning just isn't cutting it. We've lost touch with our first love: Christ. We're exhausted physically, frazzled emotionally, and parched spiritually. We need an extended time of renewal in every sense of the word.

I'd like to encourage you to take a five-day spiritual retreat. Alone. Yes, girlfriend, that's what I said: *five days alone!* No whining kids, inquisitive husbands, nagging bosses, gossipy workmates, chatty friends, borrowing neighbors, nosy mothers. . .just you and your loving Papa God. I call it a He & Me Retreat.

The concept may be shocking to you at first, but consider the myriad of benefits: uninterrupted time to get to know yourself again, to touch base with the marvelous creation Papa God made in you. It's an opportunity to relax and enjoy His rejuvenating presence, to revive your enthusiasm for the Word—a simple, uncluttered occasion to fall in love with Christ all over again.

There are numerous examples in scripture of Jesus stealing away alone for prayer and renewal; some of His favorite retreat sites were the mountains (see Mark 6:46) and the seaside or lake (see Matthew 13:1). I believe that's because He knew being imbedded in our Father's pure, unmarred creation—away from the hustle and bustle of everyday life—is the most conducive environment in which to commune with the heart of the Creator.

I know, you're thinking right now, *How could I possibly afford to take off five days to go somewhere by myself?* Honestly, sister, I don't think you can afford *not* to! Do you really think you can keep up your race-car pace indefinitely with no pit stops? Your gas tank needs refueling and your tires need re-inflating if you plan to go the distance.

It's time to get your bad self down, to do what's best for *you.* Take full responsibility and stewardship of maintaining the body, soul, and spirit entrusted to you by your Creator. So why not take the plunge? Surprisingly, your world won't stop rotating if you check out for five days. And you'll be so much better for your world when you return!

This idea isn't original—women do it all the time. There are lots of retreat centers that cater to just such personal getaways. You can Google *spiritual retreats* to find something nearby. Doesn't have to be expensive; friends or family may be willing to loan you the use of a beach condo, lake cottage, or mountain cabin for a few days and you can take your own food to avoid constantly eating out.

I was recently fortunate to enjoy just such an adventure—and that's exactly what it was: a spiritual adventure.

I spent five days in a secluded mountain cabin, alone (except for the company of my mini-poodle, Fenway) before my family arrived

for a second week together. Intentionally avoiding distractions, I had no access to TV or Internet unless I drove down the mountain into town, although I did have a DVD player and a hefty supply of chick-flicks for velvety mountain nights.

So what does one do on a five-day spiritual retreat?

Well, for the first day, I pretty much sat in a stupor, numb from the exhaustion of everyday life that had followed me like a clinging shadow. With glazed eyes, I simply took in the quiet mountain beauty surrounding me: chipmunks playing chase across dirt paths; brown field bunnies tentatively spying on me across a meadow; humming-birds checking out their red and yellow feeder, like little hovercrafts; and three bird species combining forces to dive-bomb a fat squirrel over a beak full of birdseed.

By the second day, my inner deep freeze began to thaw through the healing magic of solitude; my sluggish senses were awakened on long prayer walks: I marveled at every shade of green imaginable in the thick forests, sunbeams warmed my skin through leafy boughs, I tasted the tangy sweetness of blueberries and blackberries popped right from wild bushes into my mouth. A pony nuzzling my neck and the bass *baa* of a wooly ram at the farm across the creek made me smile. I drank in the scent of a bouquet of wildflowers picked from a sun-drenched meadow: cheerful daisies, purple asters, hearty yarrow, black-eyed Susans, delicate Queen Anne's lace.

I came *alive*! It made me realize how mostly dead I'd been.

Each morning I picked out a scripture of the day, choosing from both the Old and New Testaments during the course of the week. Reading the passage aloud a minimum of five times, I looked it up in different translations and meditated on it all day long. Picking apart each word and phrase, I used commentaries and Bible dictionaries

to research Hebrew and Greek meanings. I kept a journal of insights and aha moments I experienced while digging deep into God's Word (many of these I'll be sharing with you in this book).

I also took a stack of Christian growth books and faith-based novels I'd wanted to read but had had no time to do so. I spent several hours each day mulling over new ideas and deeper tenets of faith offered by such spiritual mentors as Joyce Meyer, Stormie Omartian, and Terri Blackstock. I adore a good, stress-relieving belly laugh, so I also included Christian humorists Martha Bolton, Rhonda Rhea, and Becky Freeman.

I felt more in tune with Papa God's heartbeat than I had in a long time.

At first, the joy of the Lord flooding my soul made me cry! Then it spilled over into a kind of delirious external expression of internal jubilation I don't usually feel comfortable letting flow around others. I danced with wild abandon in the cabin's living room to mountain music played by dulcimer, fiddle, mandolin, string bass, and banjo. I lifted up uninhibited praise as I flew over rocky creek beds and climbed steep terrain on my four-wheeler, Sir Lancelot. I burst into song during daybreak mountain walks (I'm an early riser), knowing my off-key praise offerings were just between me and my heavenly Father. . .and a curious raccoon eyeing me from behind a tree.

You, too, can create your own praise song—it certainly doesn't have to be elaborate or professional quality. . .or heard by any other human, for that matter. Papa God will love it! And what an intimate form of worship—knowing that nobody else at any time in the history of the world *has* ever or *will* ever lift up a song to his or her Creator with exactly the same words or melody you've concocted. Try it sometime! Here's one of mine:

Sunrise Praise Serenade
(Inspired by Psalm 118:24)

Feel the sweetness of the morning sunshine
Pouring through the filter of the rustling leaves,
Spreading over me a warm and fuzzy niceness
Through the pleasing tickle of the gentle, sweet-smelling breeze.

Hear the lilting harmonies of the morning
As the singers and musicians start to tune up their songs;
The humming and the drumming of the little bush beasties
As the Maestro starts the rhythm section swingin' along.

The spiders are plucking their dew-touched harp strings
As the woodpeckers start a'poundin' out that bass;
Then all at once the strong, clear tones of pipes and woodwinds
As the birds spring forth with singing from all over the place.

Chorus: For this is the day that the Lord has made.
Rejoice and be glad, so glad!
Rejoice, rejoice, rejoice; don't be sad in it, no!
Praise the Lord and be glad!

These sights and sounds sparkle all around me
As the majesty of Your creation makes my heart swell;
That little song down in my soul that is sometimes hidden
Pours forth all day with adoration, clear as a bell.

It's a razzle-dazzle opening scene, Lord,
To this beautiful, song-filled day You've made.
I've got to use this precious blessing far more often,
My lifetime ticket to Your Sunrise Praise Serenade!

Of course, on my retreat I enjoyed some cool girl stuff, too—casually exploring quaint mountain villages and craft shops, sampling fudge flavors, perusing antiques, stopping to eat an ice cream cone while watching a bubbling stream flow under a covered bridge. No hurries, no worries, nobody's needs to attend to.

And that leads me to another surprising discovery I encountered on my retreat: the realization that during decades of taking care of my family's needs and desires, I'd lost touch with my own. It was quite an eye-opener to find myself standing in the middle of a grocery store, completely befuddled about what food to purchase for just little ol' me. Everything I picked up was the preference of my husband or one of my kids; what exactly was *my* favorite? I didn't know!

It even took six sample spoons in the ice cream shop before I figured out *my* flavor. Okay, so maybe that part wasn't completely random, but it sure was fun!

Anyway, the point is that self-rediscovery is a marvelous thing, especially when you know to whom to attribute the pleasure of getting reacquainted with the charming, captivating gal He created. *You!* Hey, just because your charm has been hibernating underground for a while doesn't mean it's not ready to reemerge. Remember those cicadas from chapter 6!

So, girlfriend, what'll it be? Keep breakneck racing like you are now and allow your bad self to just get badder, meaner, and more

out of spiritual alignment. . .or do whatever you must to arrange an extended time of personal revival with your Lord? Trust me, if you put it off, it'll never happen. Schedule your He & Me Retreat today. I guarantee you'll never regret it.

> *Lord, save us all from a hope tree that has*
> *lost the faculty of putting out blossoms.*

> Mark Twain

Taming the Beast

1. Has there been a time when you felt as if you'd lost touch with your first love—Jesus?
2. Have you ever taken a He & Me retreat? Would you consider getting your bad self down and taking one now?
3. If you're not convinced, how about doing this? Divide a sheet of paper into two columns. In the first column, list all the reasons why you shouldn't take a retreat; then, in the second column, list all the reasons you should. I'll bet you three chocolate-frosted donuts that the "shoulds" win!

Chapter 11
Picky-Choosey

(Discernment)

The wise in heart are called discerning.

PROVERBS 16:21 NIV

For lack of table space, I laid out all the fixings for eight gift baskets on the floor of my home office, goodies such as cute little fall scarecrows, flavored tea bags, floral stationery, various writing supplies, and ceramic fall mugs filled with Hershey's Kisses, Godiva Gems, Baby Ruths, Nestle Crunches, Butterfingers, Dove dark chocolate–caramel nuggets, and Tootsie Rolls.

Imagining how excited the drawing winners at my writing retreat were going to be when they received these awesome prizes, I assembled all the goodies into the elegant wicker baskets and had just begun to wrap the first with clear cellophane gift wrap when I noticed the time.

Yikes! I'm late for church! I'll have to finish when I come home. Without another thought, I dropped my scissors and coils of colorful curling ribbon, grabbed my Bible, and rushed out to the car.

When I returned home two hours later, the first hint that something was wrong assaulted me in the form of a crumpled Godiva wrapper peeking out from beneath the couch. *Now where did that come from?*

I was clued in by one glance at my little poodle dude, Fenway, skulking away with a candy bar protruding like a cigar from his mouth.

"Fenway! You *bad* dog! Did you get into my gift baskets?"

Of course he had. The little choco-dickins. A chip off the old block.

A chocolate chip off the semisweet block, that is. Now lest you fret or call PETA on me, I'm well aware of the dangers of dogs and chocolate. I assure you that the little thief survived this ordeal unscathed. (I unearthed his hidden stash before he had a chance to partake of more than a nibble or two.)

The extraordinary thing was that Fenway, who normally engages in an indiscriminate dinnertime feeding frenzy, not unlike famished, flesh-ripping sharks, had carefully nosed his way through the bounty of ever-so-sweet options laid conveniently out before him and ferreted out only the best. Nothing but the Godiva and Dove bars were missing.

"You should be so discerning!" my friendly thighs whispered to each other as I chased my delinquent dog.

"Teach me good discernment" (Psalm 119:66 NASB). I'm pretty sure the psalmist wasn't talking about chocolate in this passage, but the point is that spiritual discernment is extremely important for Christ-followers. So important that the Bible says we should desire it. Yearn for it. Pray for more.

What exactly is *spiritual discernment*? It's the ability to analyze, understand, and judge from an enlightened perspective what is and is not from God. Thankfully, the Lord knew how confused we can get when we're so inundated with things *not* from God in the course of our every day, so He sent a Helper—the Holy Spirit—to enable us to distinguish the difference.

Discernment is one of the spiritual gifts listed by the apostle Paul in 1 Corinthians 12:10: "to another [is given] discerning of spirits" (NKJV). According to *The Illustrated Bible Dictionary*, this type of discernment went hand in hand with the spiritual gift of prophecy and enabled the Corinthian believers to distinguish whether prophecies uttered in church were fake or genuinely from the Lord.

"What we have received is not the spirit of the world, but the Spirit who is from God, so that we may understand what God has freely given us" (1 Corinthians 2:12 NIV). Yes, the Holy Spirit reveals the difference between truth and untruth to us, for "the Spirit searches all things, even the deep things of God" (1 Corinthians 2:10 NIV). The Greek word *apolalupto* (from which *apocalypse* is derived) means "to pull the covers back; to make bare" and is used in this passage to describe how the Holy Spirit empowers us for discernment.

He pulls back the covers. He exposes lies. And when worldly untruth masquerading as God's truth is uncovered, its nakedness is hideous indeed.

In modern vernacular, the Holy Spirit is our spiritual search engine. Our supernatural Google. Because our own world-diluted judgment isn't altogether trustworthy, we must engage His willing services, tap into His vast database of truth versus clever lies, in order to practice good spiritual discernment.

And practice we must! Practice is essential in honing any skill. When I was a young piano student, my teacher would always say, "Practice makes perfect," and it's no less true with spiritual matters. "For someone who lives on milk is still an infant and doesn't know how to do what is right. Solid food is for those who are mature, who through training have the skill to recognize the difference between right and wrong" (Hebrews 5:13–14 NLT).

But no matter how practiced we are, making the right choices based on spiritual discernment isn't easy. Sometimes it's downright painful.

As a young mother, I was in a four-woman Bible study for three years. We were all in our early thirties and became very close as we studied God's Word together weekly, often laughing hysterically through weekend get-togethers with our husbands and children. For our tenth wedding anniversary, Chuck and I renewed our vows, and my three dear Bible study sisters were featured prominently in the pictures.

Then the nightmare began.

It came to light that one of the girls—one of my dearest friends, mind you—had been having a secret affair with a business associate for over a year. She decided to divorce her husband and wanted her Bible study friends (us) to participate in her wedding to the new husband. She was pregnant with his baby.

I was devastated. The shocking revelation made me physically sick. I felt confused and betrayed. Above all, I was grieved that all those years I'd invested in spiritual growth alongside this woman, whom I thought I knew and certainly loved, had resulted in such poor discernment on her part.

And now it was time for some serious discernment of my own. I was torn; the devoted friend side of me wanted to support her, but the daughter of Yahweh embedded in my spirit knew it would be wrong to condone actions that defied God's Word.

I fasted, prayed earnestly, and sought the Holy Spirit's guidance. As agonizing as the decision was, I finally told my friend that, although I would always love her, in good conscience I couldn't take part in her wedding. I knew our relationship was at risk, but I chose to follow God's leading and leave the outcome in His hands.

Sadly, she severed all ties with me, as well as the other two girls, and disappeared into her new life. I shed countless hot tears over the loss of this precious sister, but God sent me peace that I'd made the right decision. I still think about her often and pray for her to this day.

God wants us to be picky-choosey about what we do, where we go, whom we hang with, the things we feed our eyes, ears, and minds, and even (shudder!) what we put into our mouths. Good discernment is crucial; choices we make today will affect all of our tomorrows.

But the encouraging news is that we're not on our own. With the Holy Spirit as our Helper, good discernment isn't just for furry, four-legged chocolate lovers!

> *Discernment is not a matter of simply telling the*
> *difference between right and wrong; rather it is telling*
> *the difference between right and almost right.*

> CHARLES SPURGEON

Taming the Beast

1. Do you ever have difficulty discerning truth from almost truth?
2. Do you feel logged in to your personal spiritual search engine, the Holy Spirit? Why or why not?
3. Good discernment takes practice to develop; how about starting right now? Is there a problem in your life for which you need to ask the Holy Spirit to expose lies and "pull the covers back"?

Chapter 12
Wassup in Your Sinkhole?

(Overcoming Adversity)

He [God] comforts us when we are in trouble, so that we can share that same comfort with others in trouble.

2 CORINTHIANS 1:4 CEV

At age six, my friend Julie was sent to live with her father when he and her alcoholic mother divorced. Julie was ten years younger than her brother and sister and grew lonely when they graduated and moved away. When her father remarried, Julie just sort of drifted like a boat without an anchor.

After a high school pregnancy and a series of bad decisions, Julie found herself at age twenty-three with two children and two divorces. Shame followed her like a dark cloud. Her father had recently passed away and, although she'd always despised her mother's drinking, she began treading the same twisted path. The time came when she reached her lowest of lows and seriously considered suicide.

Something made Julie call her mother one last time.

To her surprise, Julie discovered that God had turned her mother's life completely around and she was truly a transformed woman. When she invited Julie to come live with her, Julie, starving for the stability of a "real" family, jumped at the chance. Six months later, Julie, too, surrendered her life to Jesus. As God continued to mend her broken heart, she met a godly man whom she married a year later. Life couldn't have looked rosier!

Then one day as Julie was cleaning out her mom's closet, she came across a box of old family videos from before her parents' divorce. In one of them, she noticed her mother standing next to a man who was flirting with her. "Who is that?" Julie asked aloud. Within her spirit, she heard a still, small voice reply, *"That is your father."*

Thoroughly shaken at this astounding possibility, Julie asked her mother about the man. "That's, um. . .a friend of your grandmother's," she stated nervously. Julie was forced to leave the issue alone when shortly thereafter her mother began having strokes and became unable to speak. During hospital visits, her mom acted as though she wanted to tell Julie something but couldn't. And then she went to heaven, taking her secrets with her.

But not for long.

Two weeks later, Julie received a letter that began, "Dear Julie, you don't know me but I have known of you all my life. You are my half sister. . . ." The woman had seen the newspaper obituary for Julie's mom and felt that it was time to tell her the truth: Julie's real father (the man in the video) was also the father of this woman and her seven siblings. He'd died several years before, and now, with all involved parties gone, Julie's "other" family wanted to get to know her.

Whoa. What a shock, huh?

We all get unexpected, blow-me-away news at times, don't we? Adversity seems to strike when we least expect it. Kind of like a sinkhole.

Here in Florida we get lots of sinkholes—earth-swallowing pits that open up unexpectedly, devouring roads, trees, and even houses. My neighbor once stepped out of his car onto the grass beside his driveway and felt his shoe get sucked off his foot. He hopped back onto the pavement and watched his loafer disappear into a thirty-foot chasm.

There are times in all of our lives when we feel as though we've been swallowed by a sinkhole. Something shakes our world, and the ground beneath our feet falls away. Our sense of normalcy is disrupted and our foundation of security splits wide open, leaving us staring up from the bottom of a deep pit at the life we once knew.

My friend Mark grew up poor, raised by a disabled single mother in a small town. His whole life felt like a sinkhole. But he knew he didn't have to stay down in that abyss. When his high school started a tennis team, Mark found an old wooden racket with no strings. He strung it with household cotton string and began learning tennis strokes from a Stan Smith how-to library book. He saved up his quarters and was finally able to buy a real racket. After practicing his backside off, he won the inaugural tennis match for the school. It was the first time he'd ever won anything.

Fueled by this success, Mark kept climbing out of that sinkhole. After graduation, he hitchhiked to a nearby town and got a temporary job at the prison there. Thirty-three years later, he retired as warden.

Tenacity. Determination. Dependency. Which of these seems incongruent with the others?

Although it would seem that *in*dependence would be more the key to clambering out of life's sinkholes, the answer is actually the opposite—dependency. We need to have a dependency on something—or Someone—larger and more powerful than ourselves to lift us out. "The one who is in you is greater than the one who is in the world" (1 John 4:4 NIV). In fact, the more *in*dependent we become, the more likely we are to stubbornly keep wallowing in our sinkholes.

Writer James Goll, a single parent of four children, is currently battling cancer and severe financial pressures after having lost his beloved wife to the disease. He says this about enduring suffering:

"At times I felt like Job. I became acquainted with some of his well-meaning friends, each of whom gave me frequent input on the reasons why we were incurring such difficulties."[10]

We all know them, don't we? Clueless people who offer unsolicited opinions or insensitive advice about the sinkhole in which we find ourselves. Some deeply care about us; others spout from ignorance what they think is "spiritual" or consoling, not considering how much additional pain their words may cause.

After my sixth devastating miscarriage, I grew impatient with people who patted my arm and casually commented, "It's the Lord's will, Debbie; you must learn to live with it," or "God works all things together for good." I began replying, "Right. Come back after *you've* been through hell and tell me it's not hot."

Okay, tact has never been my strong suit.

It wasn't that I didn't believe in God's sovereignty or that I shunned Romans 8:28; it just wasn't the right time to have it shoved down my throat (at least that's what it felt like). My pain was raw and exposed. As truthful as their words might be, I wasn't at a place in the healing process where I was able to assimilate them into my anguished heart. I learned the hard way that the best consolation for acutely suffering people is to simply be there with them, saying nothing with words but everything with tender touch and quiet service.

Sinkholes tend to make us rigid, don't they? Fear of never escaping that bedeviling pit causes our inner modeling clay to become rock hard. We forfeit flexibility in the Master Potter's hands as we wrestle Him for control. We become resentful and fight the changes that our loss elicits.

James Goll wisely observes, "The truth is, whether we embrace it or not, things will change. To transition more smoothly, we must

be open to new things, new revelations, new places and even new connections."

What if our faith wavers? That's the million-dollar question, isn't it? Mine did. During two long years of depression following my miscarriages, I struggled mightily within my sinkhole. For every inch I made clawing my way upward, I felt like someone threw a shovel full of dirt on my head.

Finally, I got fed up festering down there. I realized that if God didn't help me, I'd go it alone. In desperation, I began listening to faith-based music and reading specific spill-your-guts psalms every day. At first, my heart wasn't in it, but I did it anyway.

Gradually, hand over hand, the Lord hauled me out of that barren crater and restored me to the land of the living. My heart engaged and began to heal.

So wassup in your sinkhole? Are you wallowing or climbing? Festering or forging a trail upward?

Here's a loving tip from your friend, Deb: When you're sick to death of clinging by your fingernails to those steep walls, just let go. Stretch your arms up and ask for Someone to reach a strong hand down to pull you up. He will, you know; you don't have to do it alone. "God is our refuge and strength, an ever-present help in trouble" (Psalm 46:1 NIV).

As a child, I used to have dreadful nightmares. I would awaken in the middle of the night, terrified and sweat-soaked. In a panic, I'd cry out for my father, whom I knew was just in the next room. Within seconds, Daddy would be there, stroking my back, whispering soft words of comfort, and soothing me back to peaceful rest.

Philippians 4:5 reminds us that "The Lord is near" (NIV). Even closer than a loving earthly father, our heavenly Father is standing by

to soothe, comfort, and reassure us.

And haul us out of our lonely sinkholes.

> *You can't run away from trouble. There ain't no place that far.*
>
> UNCLE REMUS, *TALES OF THE SOUTH*

Taming the Beast

1. Which sinkhole in your life has been most difficult for you to escape?

2. Go back and read 2 Corinthians 1:4 at the beginning of this chapter. What are some ways your own sinkhole experiences could help others?

3. Consider the term "ever-present" in Psalm 46:1. How can this scripture help when the next sinkhole threatens to swallow you?

Chapter 13
Playing Chicken with a Duck

(Achieving Goals)

I can do all things through Christ who strengthens me.

PHILIPPIANS 4:13 NKJV

As I was driving down a narrow country road beside a lake one sizzling summer afternoon, I spied something moving just ahead. Partially obscured by tree shadows, it wasn't until I was nearly upon it that I recognized a fat black-and-white duck waddling toward me down the center of the road.

I squealed to a stop about ten yards in front of the squat quacker but, undaunted, she just kept bringing it. (I assume female gender here because she acted as illogically as I often do.) When she wouldn't deviate from her preferred route, straddling the center line, I laid on my horn. All she did was stop, stick her stubborn little bill in the air, and park her feathered derriere right there.

Unlike me, she had no pressing engagements, no itinerary, no deadlines to meet; we could be there all day.

What was wrong with this ornery chick? We both obviously felt we were in the right—that each one of us had more reasons to own the road than the other. But here's a two-ton van versus a five-pound bird and she thinks she can win? Steel and chrome versus webbed feet and tail feathers? Get real!

As we stared each other down, halted at an impasse because neither party was willing to give an inch, it occurred to me that I was witnessing a metaphor of my life.

How many times am I rendered immobile by silly obstacles that I allow to hinder the pursuit of my life goals? Obstacles of my own making or even small speed bumps that I allow to swell to disproportionate size until they loom over me like the Alps?

The thing blocking my path might seem like an impassable precipice to me, but in reality, it's the size of a duck.

In my first futile efforts to remove this ridiculous roadblock, I discovered that horns wouldn't work, size didn't matter, time was not a factor, and rank was irrelevant. Lots of things *didn't* work, but there turned out to be one thing that *did*. It just took a little sweat to discover it. I finally had to climb out of my nice, air-conditioned car into 95 degree heat, walk right up to the obstinate entrée, nudge her with my foot, and then do an impromptu two-step to avoid her snapping beak. Using a stout stick, I herded her back to the pond as she squawked her annoyance the entire way.

Setting goals are important, don't you think? Goals are steps on the ladder to success. Ya gotta have them to keep climbing. When we care enough about achieving something, it's downright amazing what we can accomplish step by step, goal by goal.

I suspect systematic goal-setting pleases our Creator, who is a God of order. "Let all things be done decently and in order" (1 Corinthians 14:40 KJV).

Since I started writing eight years ago, goal-setting has made a huge difference in my life. It decreases my stress level and increases my productivity by adding structure to an otherwise crazy, flying-in-all-directions day, juggling work, writing, family, and friendships. In fact, I don't roll out of bed in the morning without reviewing my goals and agenda for the day. They aren't elaborate—maybe something like this (after, of course, my routine morning prayer walk, breakfast, and funny papers):

1. Answer e-mail 7:30–8 a.m.
2. Edit chapter 9 and finish researching next chapter 8–9:30 a.m.
3. Do evaluation at the rehab clinic 10–11:30 a.m.; call girl-friends; have lunch.
4. Write three new pages by 3 p.m. Nap or die trying.
5. Defrost and bake stuffed chicken breasts for dinner.
6. Spend evening with family.

Simple? Yep. Achievable? With a little forethought. Effective for getting me out of bed and sending me off in the right direction? You betcha.

What is your average daily agenda like?

It's essential to set realistic short-term daily goals—like baby steps—on the journey to achieving long-term goals, or you'll get frustrated and throw in the towel before you reach the finish line.

In my case, long-term goals include completion of the books for which I've signed contracts, fulfilling the requirements of my occupational therapy employer, keeping my household running, and staying on speaking terms with my family and friends. To preserve my long-term physical health, I throw in exercise (tennis) three days a week and bicycling as often as possible.

So what are your long-term goals? You likely have them, whether you realize it or not. How about taking a moment to identify them?

Years ago, I learned in a college business course about SMART goals used by successful businessmen and women. SMART is an acronym for specific, measurable, achievable, relevant, and time-based.

If you think about it, my simple daily short-term goals include all those things: a *specific* and *measurable* number of pages I need to write, tasks that are *achievable* and *relevant* to my work and family, and a set *time* for completion.

Does this sound like something you can adapt to better define and fine-tune your goals? It's not hard at all once you get into a goal-setting mind-set. And it gives you a better idea of which fat ducks need prodding to accomplish your God-ordained mission.

May I share with you six doable steps for moving the ducks blocking *your* path?

1. Want your goal enough to persevere. Face it, girl, there *will* be unexpected interruptions in your day. Plan on it. Ducks, wild moose, and dead skunks will pop up all over your expressway, and it's up to you figure out how to get around them. Your first efforts may not succeed, but *keep at it* until you've cleared the pathway.

2. Picture the end of the road. It helps so much to visualize achieving your goal—to believe that it *is* feasible and it *is* possible. Many people keep a picture of their goal posted in a visible place so they're re-motivated by it every day. Taped to my computer desk is a photo of an ecstatic me flashing my very first writing contract. On hard days when rejection dominates, that picture reaffirms God's calling for me to write and reminds me that if He wills it, He fulfills it, regardless of obstacles.

3. Create a plan. Remember, where there's a will, there's an idiot. You don't want it to be you. (I discovered this gem while trying to back my car up a one-way street.) Think through which

action steps are necessary to achieve your goal; include regular reviews to monitor your progress and make adjustments as needed. For example, to achieve my goal of losing twenty pounds (I ended up losing forty but my initial goal was twenty), I made weekly and monthly goals, and weighed myself every morning. The numbers on that scale alerted me immediately if my resolve was slipping and motivated me to *do* something about it before the runaway wagon rolled too far down the hill.

4. Pen your plan and read it aloud. Writing down goals is like making a contract with yourself; somehow your level of commitment feels deeper, and the act of verbalizing half-gelled thoughts and ideas helps pull them together cohesively. I like checklists for my daily goals—there's just something about checking off accomplishments that makes me feel warm and fuzzy all over. It's also a great idea to mark deadlines on your calendar, including incremental reminders of approaching deadlines (e.g., "two weeks till project due!").

5. Share your goals with a trusted friend. Support and account-ability help keep your goals from slip-sliding away if you somehow lose the vision.

6. Celebrate victories, no matter how small. Reward yourself when you hit a goal—you deserve it! And include your girlfriends! Break out the tiaras, confetti, and hula hoops. We don't celebrate nearly enough in this life. When I send off a completed manuscript, I buy myself a new hat! Life's short, baby—party hardy!

So the next time you're rendered inoperative by a twenty-foot brick wall, or even a spunky ducky blocking your path, remember Lewis Carroll's timeless Wonderland conversation between Alice and the Cheshire Cat (sadly, it wasn't Johnny Depp):

"Would you tell me, please, which way I ought to go from here?"

"That depends a good deal on where you want to get to," said the Cat.

"I don't much care where. . ." said Alice.

"Then it doesn't matter which way you go," said the Cat.

Hey, sister, where you go from here *matters*! Determine your destination (goal) and aim yourself in the right direction!

> *The discipline of writing something down*
> *is the first step toward making it happen.*
>
> LEE IACOCCA

Taming the Beast

1. What is the duck blocking your path today? How do you intend to move it?
2. How SMART are your daily goals? Take a moment and review the acronym so you'll remember: specific, measurable, achievable, relevant, and time-based.
3. Now how about jotting down your goals for this week? This month? This year?

CHAPTER 14
Soul'ed Out

(Raising Self-Esteem)

But you, LORD, are a shield around me,
my glory, the One who lifts my head high.

PSALM 3:3 NIV

The cool, early-morning mountain air sparkled around me. Sunbeams filtered through tree branches overhead, slanting to kiss the mossy forest floor. The beauty registered in my brain but not my heart. I felt nothing.

Nothing.

Traipsing up the remote trail above our Smoky Mountain cabin, I was too lost in my own head to be touched by the indescribable beauty of God's handiwork. Battered by a series of painful confrontations, I could only wallow in all the things wrong with me, my shortcomings, those glaring flaws that just didn't measure up to the people—those *perfect* people—that I had mounted atop my pedestal. My role models.

To avoid feeling like a failure, I'd simply stopped feeling. Just turned off the faucet of emotions. Sold out to the fear of inadequacy that held me hostage. Numbness seemed preferable to self-disappointment. Inferiority. Worthlessness.

Veering off the rocky path, something nestled between blackberry thickets and rambling rhododendron caught my eye. There, isolated from civilization where no human eye should have chanced to behold it, grew a lone lily. It was truly exquisite. The hand-sized orange and gold flower was the replication of a glorious sunrise. Whimsical brown freckles dotted ribbon-like petals that were peeled back into a perfect bow. The four-foot-tall stem curved downward just below the bloom, as if the flower were bowing its head.

How on earth did a lily bulb get way out here?

"You're so beautiful!" I addressed the startling explosion of color in the midst of muted earth tones. I cradled the delicate blossom in my palm, its face bent toward the earth, and gently lifted it upright. "You should hold your head up. You have so much to share."

Suddenly, unexpectedly, I *felt*. The emotions I'd bottled up for so long erupted like a gushing fire hydrant. My eyes flooded with tears as my heart flooded with longing. It was as if Papa God were speaking directly to me through my own words.

"You're so beautiful. You should hold your head up. You have so much to share."

I stayed there for what seemed like hours, weeping a soul-cleansing torrent with the lovely mountain lily, my unexpected heavenly messenger. As the sun rose, my little friend gradually straightened. I realized that just as this lily of the field lifted its head to draw light and life-sustaining strength from the sun, so I need to keep my face turned to the *Son*—Jesus—my own source of light and life in the darkest places. This very light and life makes me beautiful and just as unique as the mountain lily. My worth, my self-esteem, is rooted in Christ, who treasures me so much that He died for me. Not the perfect me—an impossible, unattainable goal—but *because* I'm imperfect and powerless to fix my flaws.

His power, after all, is perfected in my weakness (see 2 Corinthians 12:9). In other words, His divine intervention is more obvious when I'm a pathetic basket case. Which is most of the time. He then gets full

credit for being God. For making the incredible difference.

Women certainly understand this principle; we know a filthy, wadded-up shirt is totally transformed when washed and ironed. No kitchen floor is cleaner than the one previously covered with muddy footprints! No legs appear smoother than those finally shaved after two weeks of neglect.

It's the same when our own efforts at cleaning up the embedded stains in our character fall short. We simply can't scrub that hard. Only our supernatural Mr. Clean can.

Because of our God-given, innate sensitivity, I believe all women struggle with sagging self-esteem at certain times in their lives. If we could only see ourselves through the *Rover* perspective.

"The what?" you say.

Okay, picture yourself rolling out of bed in the morning. You are grumpy, frumpy, and have bed hair, dragon breath, no makeup. Yuck. But what does your precious doggie do when he sees you? He wags himself into a frenzy, that's what. He's chock-full of slobbery, devoted, unconditional adoration. For you. In his eyes, you are the most beautiful person in the world. Rover doesn't care about all that frumpy, grumpy stuff; he doesn't even see that other stuff—he loves *you*; he sees *you*, the real spirit-core *you*, not what you own or what you look like.

We need to start viewing ourselves like Rover does: entirely loved and entirely lovable.

God certainly sees us that way: "I have no interest in what you have—only in you" (2 Corinthians 12:14 MSG). He loves us carte blanche, the whole enchilada, stripped down, unenhanced, raw. He's not shocked or offended by anything we say or do. He loves us anyway.

And He wants us to love ourselves, too. We *can* love and respect ourselves if we make the deliberate decision to turn over to Him our

fragile feelings, insecurities, and doubts. Hand them over. Leave them in a pile at His feet.

At a recent wedding, I observed a heavyset college-age girl slip quietly into the restroom just before the bride threw her bouquet. My heart broke for this "unclaimed blessing" as she intentionally tarried to wash her hands once, twice, then a third time while cheers and laughter drifted beneath the door. She peeked out to see who caught the bouquet, then patted her hair and smoothed her skirt before taking a deep breath and returning to the celebration.

I suspect we all have memories of the times we, too, chose to shrink into the background, or disappear altogether, because we thought we didn't measure up.

An extreme example is the thirty-five-year-old Kansas woman who hid herself away in a bathroom for two years. Each day when food was brought and she was asked to come out, she replied, "Maybe tomorrow." She made headlines because after sitting on the toilet for so long, her skin actually grew around the seat, which had to be surgically removed.

None of us is perfect. Flaws will always be with us. But that doesn't mean we aren't lovely in our own right, and shouldn't hold our heads up and share the gifts and abilities we do have.

I don't want to be sold out to fear of inadequacy or society's standards of worth. Do you? No way! We'd rather be soul'ed out to the Master Creator who made us in His image and cherishes us even more than a beautiful lily on a lonely mountain.

Success is not final, failure is not fatal;
it is the courage to continue that counts.

WINSTON CHURCHHILL

Taming the Beast

1. Have you ever reached a point of turning off your feelings? Why?
2. Can you identify with the girl in the restroom, sitting out the bridal bouquet toss? What about that story resonates with you?
3. How about beginning today to look at yourself through the Rover perspective of self-esteem?

CHAPTER 15
Patching the Leaky Cauldron

(Conquering Guilt)

There is no condemnation for those who belong to Christ Jesus.

ROMANS 8:1 NLT

The morning started not with a bang, or even a whimper, but more like a cracked cauldron of hot, sticky guilt leaking into the hollow places inside my heart.

I was speaking at a women's tea in a nearby city later that morning, so I indulged in a quick peek at my e-mail before hunkering down to practice my speech. I was floored to see a response from an old friend I hadn't heard from in over five years. She'd replied to my Facebook comment about my impending wedding anniversary. Although we lived on opposite ends of the country, Linda was one of my bridesmaids and we'd upheld and supported each other through our weddings, as well as the early challenges of marriage and raising children.

I had long puzzled about the abrupt, unexplained halt of communication when Linda stopped responding to my cards, phone calls, and e-mails. But suddenly there she was online as if nothing had happened.

"Linda, is that really you?" I hastily responded. "I thought you'd died and gone to heaven! Where've you been?"

Linda confessed that she'd been nursing wounds from a comment I'd made five years ago.

Five years! And for all that time, I hadn't a clue it was me who had caused the rift. What a waste of what might have been a thriving, vital relationship that could have benefited us both. Misunderstanding and resentment had stolen joy and blessings from something as rare, pure, and precious as friendship.

How very tragic. How very sad.

Pride tried to rear its ugly head and convince me that unintentional sin isn't really sin at all, but the Holy Spirit stood firm that "whatever is not from faith is sin" (Romans 14:23 NKJV). I realized that, knowingly or not, I had lacerated Linda with the razor that is my tongue, and her pain was my responsibility. A cut bleeds the same whether inflicted by accident or intention.

I felt a tidal wave of guilt crash over me.

Do you know that feeling? I suspect you do.

Sure, we all make mistakes—some knowingly, some not. We inadvertently hurt people at times. "It only takes a spark, remember, to set off a forest fire. A careless or wrongly placed word out of your mouth can do that" (James 3:5 MSG). We let people down, trample feelings, don't live up to expectations. But it's not just careless or bad behavior at stake. Make no mistake, sister, guilt is a spiritual battle.

Many of us are spiritually schizophrenic like the apostle Paul in Romans 7:15: "What I don't understand about myself is that I decide one way, but then I act another, doing things I absolutely despise" (MSG).

And then guilt sets in like wet cement.

Even when we ask forgiveness, sometimes our guilt brakes don't engage, and self-persecution just keeps barreling full speed ahead. That's when we have to allow Papa God to override the gears and stall out our revving self-condemnation engine with His supernatural grace.

The way I see it, guilt generally falls into two categories: *ice cream* and *I-scream*.

Ice-cream guilt is a legitimate, logical, emotional response to a behavior that, deep down inside, we know needs to change. An action or habit that is harmful or wrong—like scarfing down an entire half gallon of ice cream in a single sitting. Or spreading gossip that causes someone pain. Or cheating on our income taxes. Psychologists call it "healthy guilt." I think of it as the Holy Spirit nudging believers toward becoming the best representatives of Christ Jesus that we can be.

Conversely, I-scream guilt is an unproductive, gut reaction to a situation you have no ability to alter. It's punishing yourself before God might. Examples are leaving for work after peeling your weeping daughter off your leg on her first day of kindergarten, the car accident you caused that resulted in serious injury to the other driver, the abortion your niece paid for with your babysitting money. Women know all too well the nagging, debilitating remorse that renders us frustrated enough to scream.

Psychologists label I-scream guilt as "inappropriate guilt" or "unhealthy guilt." I call it Satan's revenge.

I-scream guilt is the devil's subtle, under-the-radar way of undermining our trust in God's sovereignty. If we won't overtly become Satan's property, he'll covertly bring us under his control by tearing us away from our faith and dependence on our heavenly Father one sleepless night at a time. We feel judged and condemned, reduced to ineffective piles of guilt-ridden mush so overcome by fear of causing *more* guilt that we become emotionally immobile. Spiritually catatonic.

So what can we do about the shackles of guilt—appropriate or not—that we drag around with us like Jacob Marley's ghost?

The first move is to distinguish friend from enemy. When we feel woman's oldest nemesis, guilt, tugging at our heartstrings, we must ask ourselves: Is this ice-cream guilt or I-scream guilt? Rational or irrational? Healthy or unhealthy? Is this coming from heaven (to mold me into becoming more Christlike) or hell (to torment and tear me apart)?

If you discern that it's ice-cream guilt caused by behavior you have the ability to change—however challenging that may be—then take steps to do so:

- Bathe that specific behavior and your desire to change in prayer; ask a trusted accountability partner to pray with you.
- Seek scriptural support for motivation and strength; write out passages like Psalm 103:12—"How far has the LORD taken our sins from us? Farther than the distance from east to west!" (CEV)—and tape them to your mirror so they're the first thing you see every morning.
- Accept responsibility for your actions and create a plan; decide *before it happens again* how you'll behave differently next time. You can't win the game without a game plan!
- Thank God for His gracious forgiveness and *forgive yourself.* As Jesus told the adulterous woman in John 8:11, "Neither do I condemn you; go and sin no more" (NKJV).

To overcome I-scream guilt:

- First recognize that tears, fears, and obsessing over circumstances will not change anything.
- Ask prayer partners to help you immerse the situation in prayer and ask God to rid you of nagging guilt each and every time it tries to rear its ugly, devilish head. Remember *who* is making you a prisoner to guilt!

- In an actual physical ceremony, rebuke Satan's hold over you and state aloud that you release the guilt that has shackled you. Let it go. Free a helium balloon and symbolically send your guilt with it right up to heaven. Papa God will know precisely what to do with it. Can you say "fiery furnace"?

You know, it's extremely important to confront guilt and determine its source. Unaddressed I-scream guilt can dictate the direction of our lives.

I was once in a three-woman Bible study led by a lovely Christian mentor I'll call Mindy. Mindy had a huge impact on my spiritual growth during the year we met together, and I was brokenhearted when her husband, a career military man, was transferred to Italy. He went on ahead to house hunt, and Mindy and their three children planned to follow in eight weeks.

One week before the moving date, I arrived at Mindy's door to help her pack and found the house padlocked and deserted. Baffled, the third Bible study member and I couldn't figure out what had happened.

Two months passed before we heard that Mindy had suddenly decided she would *not* go to Italy, sent her husband word she was filing for divorce, and moved to a city across the state to pursue a relationship with an old flame she had rekindled at her recent high-school reunion.

Through a little sleuthing, I was able to learn Mindy's whereabouts and tried to contact her. She only responded once to say that she was ashamed of herself and simply could not face the spiritual accountability of seeing us again. She was consumed with guilt that she just couldn't shake.

I wanted desperately to shout, "But God will forgive you and so will we!" But she ignored all further communication attempts. I still pray that one day she'll be able to defeat that viscous inner ogre of self-condemnation and I, for one, will welcome her back with open arms.

We do ourselves no favors by rolling like little pigs in the mud of guilt over our mistakes. Staying in the pigsty is not what God intends for us to do. Once we ask forgiveness for our wrongs, He wants to morph us from filthy piglets into majestic eagles so that we can soar high above the nasty mud holes, our wings supported by His very breath.

It's just plain dumb to refuse the wings and keep our snouts immersed in slop. Yet, for some inexplicable reason, we sometimes choose to do it anyway.

Okay, to finish my opening story on a happy note, I did ask forgiveness from Linda for my careless words and she graciously forgave me. Then I forgave myself and moved on. I vowed I would not revisit that boiling brew of scalding guilt that threatens to seep into the souls of women and scorch our vibrant faith.

How about you? Is your guilt cauldron oozing something vile and rancid?

Forgiveness not only initiates a relationship-healing process, but also welds a hefty patch once and for all on that leaky cauldron of guilt.

Food, love, career, and motherhood, the four major guilt groups.
CATHY GUISEWITE

Taming the Beast

1. Girlfriend, do you have any guilt leaks that need patching today?
2. What's boiling in your cauldron? Is it ice-cream guilt or I-scream guilt?
3. So what will you do? Deal with that guilt once and for all and start flying, or keep wallowing in the mud? C'mon, girl—take the wings!

CHAPTER 16
Sneaking Up on Ourselves
(Finding Beauty in Rest)

"Are you tired? Worn out? Burned out…? Come to me. Get away with
me and you'll recover your life. I'll show you how to take a real rest."
MATTHEW 11:28 MSG

One chilly January morning a few years ago, faint, exquisite tones
interwove with commonplace commuter noise in the Washington,
DC, Metro station. A nondescript young man dressed in a baseball
cap, black knit pullover, and jeans stood against a wall, violin case open
at his feet, playing his heart out for an hour as roughly two thousand
folks rushed by.

Only seven people—that's about one every ten minutes—paused
to listen for a few brief moments. The rest hurried on their way, some
glancing at the source of this interlude of beauty in an unbeautiful
place, others not making the effort to turn their heads at all.

Can we blame them, you and I? They were preoccupied with
the minutiae of their lives, just like us: schedules, deadlines, responsibilities. . .go, go, go, do, do, do. But in their zeal to reduce their
own checklists, they had no clue what incredible beauty they were
missing.

The violinist was Joshua Bell, one of the world's finest classical
musicians. He was playing a violin worth 3.5 million dollars, only days
after enthralling a sold-out theater audience at 100 dollars a head. The
casual subway concert was a *Washington Post* experiment posing the

question, Do people recognize beauty in an unexpected context?

Sadly, it appears the answer is a resounding no. That is, unless we can train ourselves to slow down enough to *notice* these rejuvenating beauty snippets as they appear in our lives through music, art, cuisine (of course I had to include food!), nature, and people themselves.

We're often so focused on reaching our destination that we arrive without realizing how we got there. Girlfriend, the journey *itself* is real life. Getting where we're going should be half the fun!

If you're like me, although I'm usually focused on my urgent agenda, I occasionally sneak up on myself and actually *see* something I've never really seen before even though I've encountered it a million times. But this time I see it with my heart. . .before my pragmatic self can talk me out of it.

The exquisite artistry of a dew-glistened spiderweb, misty early-morning sunbeams reaching toward earth like the Almighty's fingers, the funny antics of a roly-poly puppy—all these things pour refreshing beauty into our thirsty hearts and bring a moment of sweet rest to our weary souls. They're one of Papa God's special grace notes. Balm for our skinned spirits. Ralph Waldo Emerson said, "Never lose an opportunity of seeing anything beautiful, for beauty is God's handwriting."

Don't you, too, delight in such interludes of beauty rest in the throes of your hectic day? Absolutely. You ache for beauty. You yearn for rest.

Of course, there are different kinds of rest and Papa God created us to need all three: physical, mental, and spiritual. Let's look at them separately.

- Physical: If you're not getting enough of this kind of rest, your body will drop subtle hints, such as the irritating chainsaw noise issuing from your drooling mouth before the first commercial break of *American Idol*. Or sitting down to pray and remembering nothing after "Dear Lord." Or the interesting maze of furrows imbedded in your cheek from the pile of unfolded laundry.

  ✦ One solution? Schedule a daily grownup time-out and take it seriously. Set a timer for fifteen minutes, or longer if possible (the timer is important so you won't worry about oversleeping or staring at the clock). Find a comfortable chair, hammock, or couch. Sit, lay your head back, close your eyes. Breathe in and out. Doze or not, your choice. Either way, your body is resting, relaxing, regrouping.

- Mental: Red-alert symptoms include confusion, fogginess, agitation, kicking the potted ficus, and screaming in the broom closet. Okay, it's time to change the scenery. Get away from where you are: Go for a spin on your bike, go-cart, black stallion, car, ATV, or unicycle—let the wind whip your hair and blow away mental cobwebs. Walk or jog around your backyard or a nearby park. Kayak down a river or soak in a bubble bath until you're pruney.

  ✦ You can train your fam to help you with this: Trust me, they *want* to avoid becoming BOOP (boiling oatmeal overflow phenomenon) victims. In my book *Too Blessed to Be Stressed,* I explain my theory that women are like pots of oatmeal; at the beginning of the day we simmer—little manageable bubbles of stress rise to the surface and dissipate. But as the day progresses, the heat escalates and the oatmeal boils higher and higher until it overflows. Hey, when my oatmeal nears the brink, my husband will actually take my bike out of the storage room and yell, "Time to ride!"

- Spiritual: Evidence that your spirit is sucked dry includes a downcast mood, dejection, and increased self-depreciation. You feel isolated, worthless, and cut off from God. Your prayers are dry and uninspired. Extended spiritual fatigue can lead to depression and hopelessness. So, girl, don't let it get to that point!

  ◇ An excellent spiritual booster is to meditate on one simple scripture per day. A good verse to start with is Colossians 2:10: "In Him you have been made complete" (NASB). Jot the verse down, take it with you, and repeat it to yourself throughout the day, considering all implications and possible meanings. By the end of the month, you'll have studied thirty different scriptures and will be amazed at how personal the Word has become. (Hint: The book you're holding is full of brief, meaty verses you can use!)

  ◇ Other effective spiritual vitamins include reading faith-based books, listening to uplifting music, and getting together with Christian friends. Several of us gals started a Friday morning Bible study in our neighborhood two years ago and it's really exploded. What a blessing to share laughs, brownies, prayer, heart needs, and to study the Bible with women from all faith walks. We learn from each other and from the Lord as friendships deepen and flourish.

Experiencing beauty is interconnected with a rested, open spirit. They often travel hand in hand. But sometimes we sabotage ourselves and miss both.

I once read about the mother of a tactilely defensive child—that's

therapy-speak for a child who doesn't like to be touched (more common than you might think!). This mom mourned that her little girl wouldn't allow herself to be held or cuddled unless she was really sick. Only during those downtimes—when she was listless and devoid of energy to fight it—would the child be willing to rest in the arms of the one who wanted nothing more than to lavish her beloved with comfort and love.

It made me think about how many times I'm too busy or preoccupied or defensive to allow my heavenly Father to snuggle with me. His arms are opened wide but I fill up my day with checking e-mail, shopping, working, cleaning, cooking—all the while running over for a token high-five or peck on the cheek via a microwave prayer before leaving Him standing there as I return alone to life as I know it.

And then eventually, operating on my own strength, I run out of gas. The color in my world fades to gray. Beauty turns to ashes in the furnace of fatigue.

Maybe Papa God actually *wants* me to finally run out of energy and become spiritually listless so that I'll sink into His lap and allow Him to slowly rock me while rubbing my back and stroking my hair. He allows me to become crispy fried and exhausted enough that I won't fight the rejuvenation He longs to give me. What kind of crazy woman would actually *resist* resting in the arms of the One who loves her more than life itself?

Gulp.

Me.

Maybe you, too.

Yet He desires only to colorize our black-and-white world and refill it with light and beauty. "Keep company with me and you'll learn to live freely and lightly" (Matthew 11:30 MSG). We have to be willing to sneak up on ourselves and rest in an unexpected beautiful moment before we can talk ourselves out of it through reason and sensibility, schedules and agendas.

Living life, after all, is a series of conscious decisions, an act of the will. So it's up to us to *choose* to slow down enough to enjoy snapshots of beauty—like impromptu violin concerts, spiderwebs, sunbeams, and puppies—that bring rest and peace to our weary souls.

Then, no matter what else comes our way, we can echo Solomon's words: "Now the LORD my God has given me rest on every side, and there is no adversary or disaster" (1 Kings 5:4 NIV).

> *Whatever you may look like, marry a man your own age*
> *—as your beauty fades, so will his eyesight.*
> PHYLLIS DILLER

Taming the Beast

1. Which type of fatigue do you struggle with most—physical, mental, or spiritual?
2. Do you, like me, sometimes have trouble actually *seeing* beauty in your life? Are the most difficult times when you're tired, run-down, or discouraged? What do you plan to do about that, hmm?
3. When was the last time you rocked, rested, and revived in your Father's loving embrace? What's keeping you from climbing up on His lap today?

CHAPTER 17

No Call-Waiting

(Powerful Prayer)

"Call on me and come and pray to me,
and I will listen to you."

JEREMIAH 29:12 NIV

I had to grin when I read about the Dutchman who bought the Master of the universe an answering machine. In an effort to improve modern perceptions of faith in Holland, Johan van der Dong created God's Hotline, which informed the caller, "This is the voice of God. I am not able to speak to you at the moment, but please leave a message."

Would you believe thousands of messages were left? Although the callers received no physical return call (Johan never listened to the messages because he believed "It's a secret between the Lord and the people who are calling"), they obviously hoped for some sort of spiritual response. *Hoped*. . .probably not *expected*.

Just like you and me.

We leave messages on God's answering machine, too, don't we? When we have something to say, it's easy to pick up the celestial hotline and spill, but somehow it's much more difficult to *expect* a reply.

Could it be that deep down inside we're afraid God might not answer? That He'll put us on *hold* indefinitely and forget about us? Maybe we think He's just too busy solving world hunger and preventing wars to take time for us. Or maybe we don't feel worthy of His attention.

But we couldn't be more wrong.

A brand-new Christian once shared with our Bible study group that he'd prayed for financial assistance and expectantly checked his mailbox every day for God's provision. An older, "wiser" believer shook his head and commented, "Beginner's mistake."

"No, no, *no*!" I wanted to shout. We should all be like this faith fledgling and boldly pray, anticipating a response. God assures us He'll give us one.

Remember when you were a little girl and you asked your mom or dad for a dollar? The first response was usually, "What do you want to buy with it?" Then he or she would determine, in the context of love and with wisdom beyond your understanding as a child, whether the consequences of your purchase would be good for you or not in your best interest. Or perhaps the timing was just off and it would be best to wait until later.

In the same way, Papa God answers *all* of our prayers, but His answer isn't always to give us *what* we ask for *when* we ask for it, or in the *way* we want it. In the context of love and with His eye on consequences we can't always comprehend, sometimes the answer is "Yes, with pleasure," sometimes, "No, dear one," and sometimes, "Not yet, My child."

Did you know there are more than four hundred Bible verses about prayer? It sure must be important if Papa God wants that badly for us to pick up what He's putting down.

Scripture offers many reasons why we should pray: to increase our wisdom and understanding (see Ephesians 1:17–18), to glorify God and to strengthen ourselves and other believers (see 2 Thessalonians 1:11–12), and to share our faith (see Philemon 1:6). The Bible even recommends where and when we should pray:

- Day or night (see Psalm 42:8)
- In the throes of busyness *and* in peace (see 1 Thessalonians 5:17)
- Amid trouble (see Jonah 2:1)
- In private (see Matthew 6:6; Luke 22:39–41)
- Away from home to avoid distractions, preferably a place surrounded by God's handiwork, like the sea or a mountaintop (see Matthew 13:1; Mark 6:46)

Many times we think of prayer as a one-way street, more of a monologue than a dialogue. Sometimes we pray like we're issuing directives through a bullhorn: "Need You to do this *now*, God!" or "Listen, Lord, I've already asked for this four times."

We tend to address the Almighty as our personal Santa Claus in the sky and dutifully recite our wish list before hanging up the holy phone with a resounding "Amen." How do you think our heavenly Father feels when we slam the receiver down? Or cut His reply off in midsentence?

So how *do* we hear God? What does His voice sound like?

God gave the prophet Elijah a very memorable object lesson about prayer. When wicked Queen Jezebel lit out on the war path for his scalp, Elijah bolted for the hills and ended up alone in a mountain cave, frantically trying to discern God's guidance.

As he stood on the mountainside, Elijah was exposed to some of earth's most powerful forces of nature. Gale-force winds shattered rocks all around him, and then an earthquake rattled his very bones. Finally a monstrous fire lit up the night.

But the Lord's presence wasn't in any of those things. Nope. Too crazy. Too noisy. Too overwhelming.

To Elijah's surprise, God was in the still, small voice that came only in the quiet after the storms. No doubt he had to strain to hear it after all that racket.

Sound anything like your life today? Are you too crazy, too busy, too overwhelmed to hear the Holy Spirit whispering to your heart? How many times have we, like Old Testament Jacob, been going about our everyday routine and suddenly realized, "The LORD is in this place, and I was not aware of it" (Genesis 28:16 NIV)?

Jesus was our best example of the importance—especially in the midst of our chaotic schedules—of finding a quiet place to listen for the Father's voice. Christ often slipped away from the clamoring crowds to find an isolated place to pray, devoid of distractions.

One of my favorite places to commune with the Lord is in my car. I call it my rolling cathedral. The prayer list in my glove compartment and praise music bouncing off the ceiling liner keep me spiritually uplifted while my eyes are earthbound. And it's a good time to listen—*really listen*—for that still, small voice while I'm insulated from everyday noise and clutter.

When my kids were little, my "prayer closet" was literally just that. I'd lock myself in my walk-in closet as the kids wiggled their fingers beneath the door. "Shoo!" I'd say. "This is Mommy's special God time." Bible in hand, I'd curl up beside my shoes and feel my spirit rejuvenate through ten precious minutes of alone time with the Lover of my soul. Today I steal away to a secluded hammock in my backyard or take a prayer walk. If I'm really feeling depleted, I'll bolt for a He & Me Retreat (see chapter 10).

What's your favorite place to steal away and pray?

You know, God is always trying to speak to us and sometimes there are dire consequences when we choose to *not* listen. Have you ever read the incredible story of Manasseh in 2 Chronicles 33:1–20? Manasseh began his fifty-five-year reign as king of Judah at the age of twelve. He chose to forsake God and not only desecrated Jehovah's temple by building altars to idols and star-worshipping there, but he practiced sorcery and witchcraft, leading his people into horrendous practices. He sacrificed his own children by fire to pagan gods and angered the Lord by ignoring Him when God tried to speak to him.

So Manasseh's enemies were allowed to prevail against him. He was captured and led away in shackles by a hook through his nose. *A hook through his nose!* Whoa, mama! I don't know about you, but the image of me sporting a giant fish hook through my nostril certainly motivates me to pay closer attention when God speaks!

Some people, especially new believers, feel uncomfortable praying because they aren't sure how to approach the omnipotent Creator of all things. And if you're not used to it, it can feel intimidating to pour your heart out to someone you can't see (although we women seem to have no problem with that on a telephone!).

So how should we pray? Our example, the Lord's Prayer, was given by Jesus in Matthew 6:9–13 and Luke 11:2–4. Notice the four main elements Jesus included in His sample prayer. I like to break them down into an easy-to-remember acronym: PRAY (praise, raise, admit, yield).

- Praise: "Hallowed be thy name" (Matthew 6:9 KJV). *Hallowed* means holy, honored, revered. A wonderful way to start any meaningful heart-to-heart conversation is by letting the person you're speaking to know how much you appreciate them. (Works great with husbands, accidentally neglected friends, and irritated mothers!) Papa God delights in our praises and acclamations of His goodness, grace, and loving-kindness. Do you truly value your relationship with Him? Tell Him so!

- Raise: "Give us this day our daily bread" (Matthew 6:11 KJV). Raise whatever concerns you have to God's ear. Petition for God's provision, help, and mercy in every crevice of your life. Petty doesn't exist. Your concerns, no matter how miniscule, are His concerns, too.

- Admit: "Forgive us our sins, as we have forgiven those who sin against us" (Matthew 6:12 NLT). Don't let crud keep accumulating in the filthy, neglected rooms of your heart. Let Jesus wipe them sparkling clean; He'll even get the corners! Start afresh by admitting you've sinned and ask the Lord to forgive your mistakes. Then, because Papa God pardons the pain you've caused Him, turn around and forgive those who've hurt you.

- Yield: "Lead us not into temptation, but deliver us from evil" (Matthew 6:13 KJV). Acknowledge that you can't avoid temptation on your own; in fact, you gravitate toward it like needles to a magnet. Ask the Lord to fill you with the power of His Holy Spirit and commit to yield to His guidance.

The bottom line is this: We pray in order to share our lives with the One who custom-created us. He knows us inside and out and takes joy in simply being with us. What a privilege it is to be on His preferred call list! He answers every single message and—hallelujah!—there's no call-waiting!

*Prayer is an integral part of my life. Every day I get down
on my knees and ask God to help me stick to my diet.
Then after I wallow around a while, I ask Him to help me get up.*

FRANK MITCHELL (AUTHOR'S DAD)

Taming the Beast

1. Why is prayer so crucial to us as believers?
2. Okay, sister, let's practice. Turn to Matthew 6:9–13 in your Bible and tailor the Lord's Prayer into your own, using the PRAY pattern. Remember, there are no rules here, just a guideline to help you freelance with a wing and a prayer.
3. How do *you* keep God's still, small voice from being drowned out in the cacophony of ringing phones, blaring TV, car horns, and intrusive noise?

Section 3:

Undergarments by Fruit of the Spirit (Not the Loom!)

The Holy Spirit produces this kind of fruit in our lives: love, joy, peace, patience, kindness, goodness, faithfulness, gentleness, and self-control.

GALATIANS 5:22–23 NLT

I think it's interesting that the first four fruits are internal; they're a result of the Holy Spirit's presence altering our attitudes. Like holy underwear, they support us where it counts and beautify us from the foundation up. The last five are external; the visible proof that God's Spirit within us is vibrant and thriving.

Some days, the fruit of the Spirit hangs low on our branches and we're able to pick, ingest, and enjoy its sweetness. But other days that fruit seems green, hard, and inedible. So how can these spiritual fruits transform us deliciously ripened girls into beautiful women of God? Read on!

Chapter 18
Is Love a Battlefield?

(Love)

Above all, love each other deeply,
because love covers over a multitude of sins.

1 Peter 4:8 niv

Who could forget Jennifer Garner's spirited rendition of Pat Benatar's "Love Is a Battlefield" as she bed-bounced with her pubescent pajama-party pals in the adorable movie *13 Going on 30*? The earnestness of Jennifer's character, an innocent thirteen-year-old inhabiting the body of a worldly thirty-year-old, made you want to sing into your hairbrush, grab the hands of your own girlfriends, and raise them high, united as warriors in the heartache of love's battlefield.

Sigh. Is love really a battlefield? I have to admit, sometimes it feels like it. Call me an incurable romantic, but I like to think love is more than a civilized war. Even more than an extended peace treaty or a mutual truce.

Love neurologists (yes, Virginia, there is such a thing) appear to agree with me. It seems recent studies have found that the euphoric pangs of new romance stimulate the production of dopamine in the brain, the same feel-good hormone that skyrockets when we scarf sweets. Scientists even postulate that falling in love can serve as an effective painkiller, triggering a surge in dopamine that could possibly replace pain medication.

How cool is that? Instead of counting out the ibuprofen, a gal

could flirt her way out of a toothache. Or take four kisses per hour until her migraine subsides.

Maybe that's why I think of love as the peach in the fruit bowl of the Spirit; it's soft, fuzzy, and grows sweeter as it ripens.

Okay, okay—enough of the gooey stuff.

Realistically, I know love sometimes *is* a battlefield. There are times when we bloody our swords and clink around the kitchen (and bedroom) in steel armor. The enemy knows just where we're vulnerable, so we hide behind thick shields to protect ourselves.

Ah, yes—the enemy. Who exactly *is* our foe?

"That's easy," you might respond. "My husband!"

But didn't we think marrying him meant we were signing up for the *same* battalion? Aren't we supposed to be teammates, comrades, trench buddies who cover each other's backs and fight side by side for the same causes? Then how come we argue so much? What's with all the midnight tears? Why does our future together sometimes look so dark?

Questions. . .so many hard questions.

In their book *Love & War,* authors John and Stasi Eldredge shed light on the war raging in our marriages. But the enemy isn't who we might think.

The Eldredges conclude that many of the skirmishes and battles we wage with our spouses are covertly instigated by our true enemy— the "father of lies" (John 8:44 NIV). Satan bombards us with subtle, worming-under-the-skin lies (that may even be partial-truths) about our spouse:

If my husband really loved me, he'd stop doing that.
He's so pigheaded—he always thinks he's right.

He never listens to me.
He knows exactly how hurtful he's being and he doesn't care.
He'll never *change.*

In the hollow echoes of our wounded hearts, the lies somehow sound completely believable. So to us, they become reality. Reality based on untruth. According to the Eldredges, "Once we buy in to the lie. . .we come under the spell and come under the influence of *that* interpretation of events. Then it pretty much. . .becomes self-fulfilling."[11]

I don't know about you, but that strikes a chord with me. I can't count how many times, while in a state of anger, resentment, or frustration, I have accepted, without a molecule of resistance, lies like:

It's useless to try.
This is as good as our relationship is ever going to get.
Just stuff it inside and live with it.
It's too hard to work at making it better.

And then those fallacies become the basis for how I relate to my husband.

But we have to remember the source of these depressing truth distortions: the great deceiver; the accuser; the one whose hell-bent goal is to destroy our marriage, the sacred union we trustingly entered in God's holy name.

And God is *his* worst enemy. We're only pawns, expendable privates Satan thinks nothing of sacrificing on the front line in his ruthless onslaught against the power of heaven.

So what's the result of surrendering to these lies about our marriage? John Eldredge admits, "I shift into autopilot. . . . I duck the major issues, hope for a cordial détente. I lose my desire for something more."

That's the tragic part.

For when you give up hope for improved intimacy with your husband (I'm talking a closeness of spirit here, not just sex), you lose the battle *and* the war. Intimacy isn't random or accidental, or even magical. You have to *earn* it, to plant, cultivate, water, and nurture seeds of trust. And fertilize them with respect, laughter, time together, shared interests, and even a few tears. And then turn it all over to the Master Gardener's loving care so that one day intimacy will sprout and grow strong and healthy.

Trust me on this one, girlfriend. After almost thirty-five years of marriage, I can attest that if you don't cave in to the lies, if you don't settle for "okay" or even "better than average," but instead keep striving for "fulfilling," your marriage can climb to levels of intimacy you never dreamed possible.

That's not to say there won't be days when you drag your She-Ra armor out of the closet, fasten your spike leggings, and sharpen your spear. Because when love's a battlefield, your marriage has an archenemy. Just remember who he is.

Sadly, that enemy doesn't just stop with our marital relationships; he wages a battle for the hearts of our beloved children through drugs, promiscuity, alcohol, and so many other lies that promise "more," "better," or "freedom."

Jennifer was a beautiful child who grew up with my children. Raised in a Christian home, she rarely missed church events. Smart, fun, and athletically gifted, Jennifer was very popular in her Christian school and a natural leader.

But something happened when Jennifer was sixteen. She began buying in to Satan's lies offering "more" in the form of alcohol. Her sense of right and wrong became dulled as she sought higher highs and crazier thrills. She became desensitized to Satan's lies and made bad choices that turned her life upside down. In college she started experimenting with pot and was soon sucked into the underworld of addictive drugs.

Jennifer's family and friends utilized every weapon they could find on the battlefield for Jen's heart. But while she was in drug rehab, the enemy deceived Jennifer into one final skirmish in her moment of weakness, and she died of an accidental overdose at age twenty.

Satan may have won that battle, but he lost the war. Jennifer had given her heart to Jesus two years earlier and is now in heaven, rejoicing with her Savior.

When Satan attacks our marriages, our children, or any other area of our lives, our first major victory is to recognize who our enemy really is. When his lies begin to burrow under our skin and itch to be noticed, we must blow his undercover identity and expose him in the searchlight of truth. He hates the spotlight. He deceives much better in the dark.

Only when our true enemy is identified and targeted do we know where to aim our ammo. Then Love Himself will win the battle for us. He already has.

*The way to love anything better is
to realize that it might be lost.*

G. K. CHESTERTON

Taming the Beast

1. So what do you think? Is love a battlefield? Why or why not?
2. What lies have you bought into related to your marriage?
3. What lies have your children swallowed? Is this something you can discuss with them? If not you, then who?

CHAPTER 19
Becoming a Lifer
(Joy)

"The joy of the LORD is your strength."

NEHEMIAH 8:10 NASB

I was raised just down the road from the state penitentiary, where my father worked for decades. Our family, along with many others, would line up at the employee cafeteria after church each Sunday, where our delicious meal was prepared and served by convicted felons.

Yep, you read that right. Felons. Prisoners. Convicts.

Sound scary? It wasn't. These culinarily gifted men took pride in their work and it showed. You could cut the roast beef with a feather, the lemon chiffon pie was to die for, and the buttermilk biscuits would melt in your mouth. We were all bummed the day the pastry chef got paroled.

These guys we came to know and appreciate were trustees—trusted inmates who had earned the privilege of intermingling with the general public. But there were other prisoners we *didn't* see—hardened criminals harbored behind concrete walls topped with razor wire and guarded by armed sharpshooters in towers. These convicts were called lifers—committed to incarceration for life because of terrible choices they'd made, many with no possibility of ever tasting freedom again.

So some would try to escape. . .and occasionally succeed.

I remember when one of my school chums who lived about a mile from the prison came home one afternoon to find her mother tied to a chair. When a newly escaped inmate had appeared at the door, her mom had pleaded with him. "Take anything you want, just please don't hurt me." So he'd bound and gagged her unscathed, helped himself to a ham sandwich, her wallet, and husband's clothes, and before he drove off in her car, even turned on the TV so she wouldn't get bored.

Once when a state politician and his large entourage arrived to tour the prison, a clever corrections officer noticed something unusual. He calmly walked over and placed his hand over the top of a barely visible pipe protruding from the ground near the gate. Within minutes, the dirt began erupting as an inmate frantically dug his way out of his underground hiding place when his airway was blocked. He'd planned to slip out the open gate when everyone was distracted.

Prison lifers are bound to a certain lifestyle because of their choices. But you know what? We, too, are lifers in a way. Because of our choices—yours and mine—we determine how we'll spend our days on this earth. Will it be on our customized death row, shackled to chains of worry, hopelessness, and depression? Or will it be a joy-filled life of freedom through Jesus?

Some time ago, I made the conscious decision to become a joy lifer—someone who *seeks* joy, regardless of her circumstances. It hasn't been easy. My blown-by-the-winds-of-circumstance self often wrestles me into a half nelson and parks its humongous fanny on my chest until I gasp, "Uncle."

But I've come to see that joy is a commitment we make, even more important than commitments like choosing a marriage partner, or political party, or profession, or church. Joy is not just an emotion, but a way of life. Not a reaction but a *transaction*. It's signing on the dotted line that we believe:

Security is not our god.

Good health is not our god.

Happiness is not our god.

God is our god. And He promises that His joy is our very strength (see Nehemiah 8:10).

So how do we morph from circumstance-controlled lifer to joy lifer?

One of the best ways is to *look for* threads of joy woven into the fabric of every day. Evidence of the joy our heavenly Father takes in His creation. Little bursts of individual sweetness, like luscious grapes in the fruit bowl of the Spirit. I call them *joy hors d'oeuvres*—a tiny foretaste of heaven, a surefire smile catcher, as delicious to your soul as smoked-salmon puff pastries to the palate.

Many of my most memorable joy hors d'oeuvres occur in my car as I dash to some important place, seeing but not *really* seeing my surroundings whiz by at 50 mph. Occasionally life unexpectedly freezes into a snapshot, a single frame of joy.

Know what I mean? I know you do.

There was the time I was tooling past a retention pond on my way to work one brisk fall morning, mentally locked tight in my little serious world, when an odd movement on the bank caught my eye. It was a carefree otter, merrily cavorting through misty early-morning sunbeams, glad to simply be alive. His freedom of expression totally moved me. I forgot my to-do list, pulled over, and with a goofy grin on my face, watched the little guy celebrate life. I connected with my Creator through His creation and felt His immense, immortal joy. My whole day felt light and cheerful.

Then there was the time I was late for an important meeting when two leggy sand hill cranes literally leaped into my consciousness. I live in central Florida, and so cranes loitering along the roadway are not all that rare, but this incident was unusual. These four-foot-tall birds launched into an utterly delightful dance recital. Must have been courting season, for they put on quite a show, hopping, springing, flitting about with attitude. You'd have thought they were auditioning for *Dancing with the Stars*. By the time I reluctantly pulled away, my spirit felt just as agile and light-footed as those graceful birds.

One of my very favorite joy hors d'oeuvres was an "aww" moment when I was cutting through a residential neighborhood. I noticed a fellow on a riding lawn mower heading straight for a woman whose back was turned as she gazed at a flower bed. For a second, my heart caught in my throat as I thought he might actually hit her, but instead, he strategically whisked her off her feet, like a cowboy rescuing a damsel in distress in an old Western, and proceeded to ride around the yard, cradling her in his lap, bellowing an out-of-tune "You Are the Sunshine of My Life."

It's these extraordinary breaks from ordinary routine that bring revitalization to our souls and beauty to our attitudes. They buoy our spirits with joy-filled life preservers, empowering us to float above the everyday muck.

Okay, this one's easy to say but hard to do: "Rejoice always" (1 Thessalonians 5:16 NKJV), one of the shortest verses in the Bible. Always be joyful—how is that possible? Are we supposed to just naively turn our backs on all the bad things that happen? Hang up on bill collectors? Ignore that breast lump? Avoid marriage counseling when our home is a conversation graveyard?

Of course not.

The problem is that we often confuse happiness with joy. Happiness is directly related to our external situation—hey, there's enough money in the bank to pay the bills this month! Are these pants actually looser? Is Junior's fever finally breaking? Hooray! The bluebird of happiness builds a nest in your lingerie drawer.

But joy comes from a deeper level: the it-is-well-with-my-soul level; the bottom-of-my-heart place where we trust the Lord enough to not only believe but actually behave like He is sovereign and *whatever* happens to us is part of His plan.

My pastor, Mark Saunders, says, "Happy sometimes doesn't come in the Christ-following package, but joy always does."

We just have to rip off the paper and unwrap the package.

Experiencing joy in the throes of hard times is something that can't be explained, really. . .it's purely supernatural. It's one of the amazing mysteries of our faith. But I can attest that it's real: When we sincerely ask the Holy Spirit to fill us with the joy of the Lord and commit to *focus on* that joy, He'll do it. We're suddenly, amazingly, miraculously overflowing with His warmth and love and hope.

Isn't that what joy really is?

J—Jesus

O—Occupying

Y—You

Then we can claim like David, "I always see the Lord near me, and I will not be afraid with him at my right side. Because of this, my heart will be glad, my words will be joyful, and I will live in hope" (Acts 2:25–26 CEV).

Joy truly is a marvelous, extraordinary place to live, and there's plenty of space for more lifers. After all, joy is the best antiaging, stress-reducing, load-lightening, inner-ogre-conquering conviction that exists. And razor wire is *not* included!

Taking joy in life is a woman's best cosmetic.

ROSALIND RUSSELL

Taming the Beast

1. To which institution are you a committed lifer—Jesus joy? Circumstances? Your own self-made death row? Or something else?
2. What was your favorite joy hors d'oeuvre ever? Do you enjoy them often? Do you prefer sweet or savory?
3. Will you join me in seeking a delicious joy hors d'oeuvre each day?

Chapter 20
Floating in the Stress-Pool

(Peace)

Letting the Spirit control your
mind leads to life and peace.

Romans 8:6 nlt

I'm a landlubber. Yes, I'll admit it—my sea legs are as wobbly as a newborn colt's. Probably has something to do with my first experience aboard a cruise ship while celebrating our tenth wedding anniversary.

Did I say *ship*? My bad. It was more like an oversized cork, bobbing up and down on the turbulent Gulf of Mexico for five days with ten-foot waves sloshing over the railings as Hurricane Gilbert completely wiped out our destination, Cozumel.

I learned very quickly what the inside of a paper bag looks like.

They aren't kidding when they call them high seas. There was nowhere to escape the storm; peace simply could not be found on that lurching boat. (Incidentally, after our ill-fated cruise, our Noah-era ark was "retired" to the bottom of the ocean. I was just glad we weren't on it at the time.)

Forget trying to sit in the tilting dining room for a meal (who could eat when your stomach is heaving harder than the tempest?), or even sprawling in your bunk. In our teeny-tiny cabin, Chuck and I had perpendicular bunks along two walls, which left about six square feet of foot space. (Believe me, trying to save thirty dollars a night for two single beds in a broom closet is definitely *not* worth it!) Every time we'd

crest a billowing wave, he'd topple over the side of his bunk and my head would bang into the top of mine. Then we'd hit the trough of the next wave and he'd get pitched into the wall and my feet would smash against the bottom of my bunk. Our beds needed seat belts!

I've never felt so helpless and hopeless in all my life. Up and down. Back and forth. Over and over, hour after hour the boat lurched, throwing our equilibrium completely off. We couldn't stagger down the hall without being hurled into a handrail. And there was nothing we could do to improve our lot. Medication and shots didn't help; they ran out of seasickness bags after the third day. Even the crew started disappearing. We could only hope someone was still driving the boat.

It was the most miserable, stressful vacation ever.

But it sure made me appreciate the beauty of peace when we finally ported. It took a full week before I got my land legs back and the earth stopped rolling beneath my feet.

After my own maritime experience, the storm that rocked Jesus' boat took on new meaning:

> *And a great windstorm arose, and the waves beat into the boat,*
> *so that it was already filling. But He [Jesus] was in the stern,*
> *asleep on a pillow. And they awoke Him and said to Him,*
> *"Teacher, do You not care that we are perishing?" Then He arose*
> *and rebuked the wind, and said to the sea, "Peace, be still!" And*
> *the wind ceased and there was a great calm.*
>
> MARK 4:37–39 NKJV

"Peace, be still." Wow. Three simple words stilled the storm, calmed the winds, and brought peace to those in turmoil. No more retching over the rails, no more floundering about while forces over which you

have no control hurl you to and fro.

Just what we hope Jesus will do to the storms in our lives.

Hey, did you notice where Jesus was during the worst of the tempest? He was in the stern, curled up on a pillow, *asleep*. Does that sound like someone panicking about His horrendous situation? Someone fearful or frantic?

Not at all. It sounds like someone who knew the outcome of the storm all along. Someone at complete peace with God and Himself, regardless of His circumstances. Someone whom I aspire to emulate.

But you know, Jesus doesn't always quell the storms of our lives, does He? Sometimes we have to experience the strength of the wind and waves before we can appreciate the peace He brings. And it might not be external peace at all; our outward circumstances might continue to surge all around us, but that doesn't mean He can't bring us internal peace in the midst of the chaos. "The LORD gives strength to his people; the LORD blesses his people with peace" (Psalm 29:11 NIV).

Sometimes Jesus calms the storm, and sometimes He calms our hearts.

An online survey by the American Psychological Association found that the majority of Americans live at stress levels up to 7 on a scale of 1 to 10, citing money, work, and the economy as the leading stressors. Whoa. That's a looong way from enjoying a life of peace!

So how do we get from 7 back to 1?

I think equilibrium is the key.

Just as the constant pitch of my disastrous cruise ship kept me off balance, losing equilibrium in our everyday lives keeps us from embracing peace. We become as dysfunctional as our off-balance washing machine doing the mambo across the floor. Or that annoying *ker-thump*, *ker-thump* of the car tire that's out of alignment. Or the

squeaky cabinet door that won't stay shut.

Let's talk about a few practical, peace-restoring steps even more effective than getting that washing machine grounded, tire rotated, and cabinet door adjusted.

- Commit wisely. It takes gumption to achieve a workable balance of your commitments, especially if you think you must meekly accept each and every project thrust your way. Cease and desist, girl! You don't have to do *everything* anybody asks you to do. You hereby have permission to say, "No!" God only sends specific responsibilities your way; the rest you add on your own. Discernment is crucial. Ask yourself: is this task a wise use of my limited time and God-given talents and abilities, or will it only add confusion to my life and detract from what I *should* be doing?

- Get back up. Remember when your little tyke discovered the fine art of equilibrium while learning to ride his bicycle? Concentration, lots of falls, and constant readjustment were necessary for him to finally find the right combination of factors that enabled him to remain upright and in control while careening down the driveway.

  - ✧ Balancing work, faith, and family takes the same kind of determination and focus. Sure, you'll make some mistakes, but after a fall you must pick yourself up, wipe the gravel off your skinned knees, and keep pedaling until you can remain upright and in control.

- Recognize your priorities. Like cut diamonds, you have many facets reflecting your multiple commitments. Facets may include marriage; jobs; children; household responsibilities;

relationships; physical, mental, or spiritual health issues; education/training; aging parents; finances; church commitments; and countless others. What are your top four priorities? Are these priorities the focus of most of your time, energy, and resources? Do you feel that any particular commitment is pulling you off balance?

- Adjust as needed. As you may know by now, tennis is my preferred form of exercise. I've played two to three matches weekly for the past fifteen years. When I lost one-fourth of my body weight, I was surprised at how much it threw me off-kilter. Without as much of me to heave around the court, my timing was off. I tripped over my own feet, overran the ball, and body-slammed my partner. We looked more like Abbott and Costello than the Williams sisters. It took weeks of practice to adjust my sense of balance.

  - ✧ Perseverance is important in establishing ongoing balance in our lives. Time constraints are fluid to the changing seasons of families, jobs, and our own evolving needs. Things consuming the lion's share of our time and energy today may not be the same next month. Or next year. We need to frequently reassess and adjust our priorities.

- Balance the seesaw. The only hope we have for enduring past lunchtime tomorrow is to put God on one side of the seesaw and everything else on the other side. He's our balance! Then we're not slammed into the ground, nor are we left flailing in the air. At last we're on an even keel. When we achieve balance, our responsibilities no longer feel overwhelming. In fact, they feel not only manageable, but fulfilling!

It's true that the storms of life can fling us about until we don't know which end is up. We may lose our equilibrium for a while, like I did on my cruise from Hades, and feel as if we'll never get off the ship.

But we can learn, like the psalmist, to "embrace peace—don't let it get away!" (Psalm 34:14 MSG). In the fruit bowl of the Spirit, peace is the banana; smooth, quiet, and understated, but full of nutrients we need to endure (between sets, we tennis players munch on bananas to keep muscles from cramping and increase our stamina).

If we turn to Jesus, He'll utter those three little words: "Peace, be still." This proclamation is our inner tube (and I do mean *inner*) to stay afloat in our stress-pools instead of drowning in them!

I'm pro-God, pro-American, pro-family, and pro-found (Ha!),
but I'm not Pro-zac!

MORGYNNE NORTHE

Taming the Beast

1. Are you weathering a storm in your life right now? Is it pummeling your outsides or insides? Or both?
2. What number would you say is your average daily stress level on a scale of 1 to 10? Where do you find peace?
3. Does any part of your life feel off balance? What can you adjust to reestablish equilibrium?

Chapter 21

Pack Up Your Patience in a Paper Bag

(Patience)

Wait patiently for the LORD. Be brave and courageous.
Yes, wait patiently for the LORD.

PSALM 27:14 NLT

Okay, who *wouldn't* want to go to a Jonas Brothers concert? Even at my age, you've gotta think they're cutie patooties. So you might have to exert a *little* patience waiting in line, but how bad could it be?

At least that's what my friend Kim thought. Functioning as a single parent to her five children while her husband was working out of state, she was exhausted and needed a pick-me-up. So she splurged on the expensive tickets for her two adolescent daughters and herself, thinking it would be a special memory-making girls' night out.

Boy, was she right. But for the wrong reasons.

As she drove toward the outdoor concert venue, with dark, ominous clouds tumbling overhead, Kim learned that the cancellation policy stated the show must go on, rain or shine. She felt uneasy about the impending thunderstorm, but she couldn't afford to lose the ticket money. Although the stage was covered, many of the seats were not. Well, surely it would be okay.

Fat raindrops turned into a monsoon-like deluge, but that didn't appear to dampen the spirits of her excited daughters, even as Kim joined legions of cars inching toward the parking area. She was directed to an unpaved lot in far, far away land and stepped out of the car into three inches of thick, black mud. That was okay, though, because the myriad of puddles, lakes, and rivers they had to wade through en route to the venue helped demuck their sandals. (They'd intentionally worn sandals to avoid miserably wet socks and shoes for the duration of the concert.)

As they joined the huddled masses trudging toward the amphitheater, Kim was suddenly stricken with the malady familiar to every busy woman: DRAT (don't remember a thing). With all the confusion of debarking in the silt sea, she couldn't recall if she'd locked the car. So back through the mud fields she plodded.

By the time she'd backtracked and rejoined the mob, Kim's feet were stinging like crazy. She glanced down to discover her sandals were crawling with ants. Knowing she was at risk of being trampled, she had no choice but to hunch over her swollen, filthy feet, blocking the disgruntled hordes funneling into line behind her as she plucked ants from between her itchy toes.

What a nightmare! Could anything else go wrong? At this point, Kim was ready to hoist her white flag and flee, but one look at her daughters' eager faces squelched that idea.

Filthy, itchy, swollen, and soaked, they finally arrived at the entrance, only to find the gates locked. A vast sea of bodies undulated around them as they waited in the miserable downpour for nearly two hours before the concert was officially cancelled.

Are you feeling Kim's pain? I certainly am. I truly believe God gives mothers an extra dollop of patience, because if He didn't, we'd all be bald, twitching, and calling our lawyers from the slammer. When our kids are young, we learn to pack up our patience in a paper bag and take it with us wherever we go.

Patience. . .the plantain in the fruit basket of the Spirit; a mature, second cousin to peace (the banana). It's that elusive virtue we're afraid to ask God for more of, lest He give us more reason to need it.

I happen to live in Tampa, Florida, the city *Forbes* magazine rated last year as number 4 among the 10 most stressful cities in the United States.[12] Factors contributing to this dubious distinction include unemployment levels, long work hours, frustrating commutes, limited access to health care, and poor physical health.

Well, mercy—it's no wonder we're so stressed out down here if you consider all the drenched, sneezing, ant-bitten women tromping through mud puddles!

And then you have the Floridians who never seem to run out of patience. Take Danny, for example. Danny was forty-four, broke, unemployed, and living in his car. One day he recalled the three meals a day, roof over his head, and real bed he had during his past life in federal prison where he'd spent five years for bank robbery. In his own words, incarceration really "wasn't that bad."

So Danny casually walked up to a Federal Credit Union teller and said, "Good morning. This is a robbery. You might as well call the police now."

Danny then calmly took a seat on the lobby couch and patiently waited.

Okay, so maybe Danny isn't such a good example of the merits of patience, but you've gotta love that story (it's true, I promise!).[13]

Patience certainly isn't for wimps. Take a closer look at Psalm 27:14 (at the beginning of this chapter). The psalmist links patience directly with courage; in other words, it takes a brave soul to employ the strength and fortitude necessary to be patient in the heat of difficult situations.

Patience is *not* passive; it's a dynamic, intentional process that grows with time, maturity, and insight. "A person's wisdom yields patience" (Proverbs 19:11 NIV).

For years, my friend Cheryl has patiently prayed for God to move in her husband's heart. One Sunday, she was weary of sitting alone in church and concerned that her husband might never be by her side. Overcome by tears as she watched other couples worshipping together, she earnestly prayed about time slipping away on her "two becoming one" heart's desire.

As she entered into God's presence in worship, three little words paced evenly through her mind: *"In My time."*

Cheryl confides, "Never before had I felt such a divine impression—this deep knowing that God cared about the deepest desire of my heart. I felt like the daughter of a protective and loving Father. To this day, I don't fret when I pray about my husband's coming-soon change of heart. Those three little words are as fresh now as then. And 'in His time' means it's an already-done deal and a perfectly sealed promise. So for now, I wait and trust, for it's simply a matter of time."

I so admire people like Cheryl who have the courage to be patient. To wait on the Lord's timing, even for something you want so badly, takes invasive bites out of your personal peace. I often take the coward's way out when I feel that I've used up my daily patience quota, and lash out in frustration. But there is no shelf life on patience.

Someone once said, "We may not all develop patience as quickly as we want, but we can learn to tolerate our impatience better."

That's my short-term goal: to tolerate my impatience better until the real deal emerges like a buttercup raising its head from a charred field. I'm constantly learning and growing, but I've still got a long way to go to achieve *real* patience.

Throwing my racquet into the net in my tennis match this very morning is evidence of that. How embarrassing. As soon as that temper missile flew out of my hand, I wished I could take it back, but it was too late.

We all have temper missiles of some kind. Oh, maybe not hurling a physical object like a tennis racquet, but some way we react with impatience when our hot buttons are pushed. It might be biting the kids' heads off when they make us late, slamming the office door on an annoying coworker, or imposing the silent treatment when Spouse forgets to take the trash out yet *again*.

What's your most recurring temper missile? What pushes your launch buttons? Do you have a countdown or do you leap directly from 10, 9, 8. . .to blastoff?

As irritated as I get with myself and others, and feel like I'm the most impatient person in the world, I find comfort in knowing the apostle Paul felt the same way about himself. "Since I was worse than anyone else, God had mercy on me and let me be an example of the endless patience of Christ Jesus. He did this so that others would put their faith in Christ and have eternal life" (1 Timothy 1:16 CEV).

My long-term goal is the same as Paul's: to point others to Christ Jesus. God's never-ending patience with me gives me the motivation to develop patience with others so that they, too, can come to know His mercy and grace.

Author Adel Bestavros said, "Patience with others is love; patience with self is hope; patience with God is faith." Just look at some of our biblical examples of faithful people waiting on the Lord's timing: Noah, waiting for rain as he toiled away on the ark month after month; Esther, waiting for years to find out how God would use her. And don't forget David who, while waiting to grow up to be a warrior, found God using him as a boy to slay a giant and change the attitude of a nation.

Papa God wants to use *us* as examples of His patience, too—yep, flawed ol' you and me. Even as we're waiting to grow up (spiritually), you never know how He might use us today, despite mud puddles, or ant bites, or temper missiles.

And, thankfully, the paper bags He offers us, in which to pack up our patience for takeout, are Outback-size!

If the person you are talking to doesn't appear to be listening, be patient. It may simply be that he has a small piece of fluff in his ear.

A. A. MILNE'S *WINNIE THE POOH*

Taming the Beast

1. Ecclesiastes 7:8 tells us, "Patience is better than pride" (NIV). How does pride hinder the development of patience in your life?
2. Are there any temper missiles you wish you could take back? Have you asked Papa God to help you dismantle the launch pad?
3. Are you in the habit of packing your patience for takeout or leaving it untouched, tucked away beneath your tablecloth?

Chapter 22
Resuscitating Dead Possums

(Kindness)

Never let loyalty and kindness leave you! Tie them around your neck as a reminder. Write them deep within your heart.

Proverbs 3:3 NLT

Pennsylvania state troopers were flabbergasted when they came upon a man kneeling beside a dead possum on the side of a highway, attempting to give it mouth-to-mouth resuscitation. I kid you not. We're not talking about a cute little bear cub or even a cuddly puppy—it was a *possum*! But don't laugh yet.

The clincher is that the man was tipsy and the animal had been roadkill soufflé for several days. You may laugh now. After you gag.

Okay, I'll admit that this is taking compassion to an extreme, but it seemed like a great way to get us thinking about kindness.

In the fruit basket of the Spirit, kindness is the kiwi; the green smiley face in your compote. The wonderful virtue that compelled Jesus to heal the lame, return sight to the blind, feed the hungry, and give lepers their lives back. And He wants us to treat each other with the same kindness: "All of you, be like-minded, be sympathetic, love one another, be compassionate and humble" (1 Peter 3:8 NIV).

Easier said than done, isn't it? Especially in a modern world where kindness is often eyed with suspicion, tender touch is avoided, and compassion is punished. Lawsuits against Good Samaritans make people think twice before offering a helping hand. Well, intelligent

people, anyway. That, of course, would exclude me.

I was driving home from a Christmas pageant around nine o'clock one chilly December night with my kids who were at the time seven and four. There were no other cars visible as I neared the top of a narrow two-lane bridge spanning a river in the heart of Tampa. My breath caught in my throat as I swerved to miss a body lying half on the sidewalk, half in the road. (Is it any wonder we won the stressful-city award?)

Anyway, with heart pounding, I pulled over on the far side of the steeply arched bridge.

What should I do? In order to check on the fallen man, I'd have to lock my children in the car alone in the dark and run back up the bridge, a defenseless woman in a seedy part of town. Saying it out loud even now sounds reckless and stupid (but you've probably already figured out that's exactly what I did).

After hastily cautioning the kids not to unlock the doors for *anyone*, I jammed the keys in my pocket and raced back up the bridge. The man was lying motionless in a pool of blood gushing from a deep cut on his forehead. As I stood gawking, trying to decide what to do, he began to moan and push himself farther onto the highway.

With the headlights of an approaching car reflecting off the bridge railings, I grabbed the guy's arm and tried to pull him back onto the sidewalk, explaining that he was hurt and must stay out of the road. He was delirious—I couldn't tell whether it was from alcohol or loss of blood—and didn't comprehend anything. We ended up in a bizarre wrestling match before he finally passed out on the sidewalk with his bloody head in my lap.

Having no cell phone on me, I used my free arm to attempt flagging down the few cars crossing the bridge at that time of night,

and finally one stopped. A wide-eyed elderly couple cautiously cracked open their window and asked if I needed help. In my state of confusion, and without thinking through the possible consequences, I gushed, "Oh yes—I don't know what's wrong with this guy but I had to get him out of the road and my kids are all alone in my car on the other side of this bridge. Can you please call the police?"

They drove away as another car approached from behind, leaving me covered in a stranger's blood and praying like crazy that I hadn't just put my children in mortal peril.

Within minutes, I heard the wail of a siren and turned the still-unconscious fellow over to the police. Running down the bridge's expanse toward my car, my panic began to subside as I saw the kind old couple sitting in their car parked beside mine, waving and making silly faces at my giggling kids.

Psalm 111:4 was infused with new meaning just for me: "The LORD is gracious and compassionate" (NASB). And kind beyond what we deserve. (By the way, this was when I learned that hydrogen peroxide works miracles on bloodstained fabric!)

Now, don't get me wrong—I'm certainly not encouraging anyone to sacrifice common sense for kindness (hey, it's no sacrifice for me—I swim on the shallow end of the common-sense pool). God absolutely does *not* ask us to put ourselves or anyone else in danger to fulfill His Galatians 5:14 mandate, "Love your neighbor as yourself" (NLT).

Kindness can be as simple as, well, loving your neighbor. Like Lynn.

Our weekly neighborhood ladies' Bible study had just gotten underway one Friday morning when Lynn from five houses down appeared at my front door, visibly shaken and puffy-eyed.

"Can you please pray for me?" she asked, her voice breaking with

emotion midsentence. "I have to put my dog down, and the pet hospice vet is coming to my house at three o'clock to euthanize him."

Lynn's beloved Chippy was nearly fourteen, deaf, and suffering from congestive heart failure. He'd begun having seizures and she knew, as shattering as the decision was, that it was time. But as all pet owners know, realizing it's the right thing to do doesn't make it any easier.

Our group of neighbor women surrounded Lynn and laid our hands on her quivering shoulders. We prayed for God to give her His supernatural comfort and peace during this most difficult time. Lynn left immediately afterward, wanting to spend as much time as possible with Chippy.

I couldn't stop thinking about Lynn the rest of the day. She was a single mom with grown kids; Chippy was all she had. My heart ached for her. As much as I *didn't* want to relive the searing pain of having to put my sweet dog, Dusty, down several years before, I knew I needed to extend to Lynn the compassionate arms of Jesus.

I cancelled my afternoon appointments and appeared at Lynn's door around two thirty to offer my presence. I couldn't do much, but I could at least be there in her time of need.

The vet was an hour late arriving, which heaped hot coals upon Lynn's heart as we petted Chippy and awaited the dreadful inevitable. But the beautiful part was that during that agonizing hour, one by one, the other gals from the Bible study group trickled in to add their support. When the horrible moment finally came, we were a cohesive prayer force.

Together we cried with Lynn and laughed through our tears over funny Chippy stories. We were, for Lynn, God's love with skin on it.

And that's kindness. On an everyday level. Christ-followers treat others with kindness. We don't wait for someone to be kind to us; we

show them how it's done. Sometimes the kindest words are unspoken.

Anyone can do it. It doesn't require special knowledge, or spiritual gifting, or extra faith. Nah. You don't even have to like possums or know marsupial CPR. You just have to be willing to open up your heart and let the compassion of Jesus pour out.

> *The best way to knock the chip off your neighbor's shoulder*
> *is to pat him on the back.*
>
> UNKNOWN

Taming the Beast

1. Look back at Proverbs 3:3 at the beginning of this chapter. Are you wearing your kindness necklace today or did you accidentally leave it in your jewelry box? It's never too late to put it on. . .it's exquisitely beautiful and matches everything!
2. Name a time when someone's kindness touched your heart.
3. Is there somebody Papa God brings to mind who might benefit from your kindness this week?

CHAPTER 23
Homecoming Queen

(Goodness)

"Whenever you did one of these things to someone
overlooked or ignored, that was me—you did it to me."

MATTHEW 25:40 MSG

"I can't believe they're here. . .and I'm going to miss them!" I stared glumly at the newspaper headline, MONKEES CONCERT TONIGHT, and then at the ugly metal brace engulfing the bandages swathing my aching left leg.

"Well, maybe they'll come back next year," my non-Monkee-adoring husband replied cheerily. His teenage years had been devoted to The Who and Creedence Clearwater Revival. Chuck shook his head at the immobilizing monstrosity that had grounded me since my painful knee surgery the day before. It had been a rough month since I'd skied upside down in the Canadian Rockies. "You're not allowed to put any weight on that leg for six weeks. There's no way you can go."

I burst into tears. Good heavens! A grown woman weeping over a Monkees concert, of all things. Must have been the Oxycodone.

Whatever the source, my tears moved my dearly beloved to action. He first got on the phone to the venue to see if there were any handicapped seats left; after purchasing the last one, he located a rental wheelchair and took off in our van to pick it up. By 7 p.m. I was happily encamped in the handicapped row abutting the stage, my braced leg sticking straight out in front of me on the elevated wheelchair leg like a battering ram.

I smiled at the young woman with Spina Bifida, seated in the wheelchair to my left, and then to the thirtysomething fellow on my right whose wheelchair was wedged tightly beside mine. He was nonverbal, except for a variety of guttural *uh, uh* noises, but seemed to understand what was said to him. As he smiled back, a little saliva dripped from the corner of his mouth. His arms were folded tightly across his chest, wrists bent and hands fisted. A tag on his wheelchair read PROPERTY OF TOMMY.

Gulp. Here I was, a fraud—pretending to be disabled for a brief time. These brave souls were the real deal, facing unimaginable struggles every single day of their lives. I felt humbled. And for some reason, extraordinarily energized.

My kids say I can talk to a brick wall (that's from trying to converse with them!), so I had no trouble striking up a conversation with nonverbal Tommy, who made up for chattiness with enthusiasm. He nodded and grunted as I told him all about my girlhood crushes on Peter Tork and Davy Jones, and the posters adorning my pink bedroom walls. His laugh was deep and heartfelt and made his whole body bounce. We hit it off just swell.

All through great songs like "I'm a Believer," "Auntie Grizelda," and "(I'm Not Your) Steppin' Stone," Tommy and I rocked out together, sharing whispers, elbow pokes, grunts, and giggles like giddy kids. And then suddenly the house lights went down and glowing cell phones went up as Davy (sans Nehru shirt, love beads, and bell-bottoms) launched into my all-time favorite, "Daydream Believer."

Across the auditorium, hands raised overhead swayed back and forth as we all sang along at the top of our lungs about the important things in life to a daydream believer and his homecoming queeeen.[14]

It was a magical moment, and I wasn't about to let Tommy miss it. I reached over and grabbed his hand, wrestled it as high as I could (which was not easy with his contracted arms), and kind of heaved both of us from side to side to keep pace with the swaying crowd.

Tommy howled with glee, his entire body bouncing with laughter as drool flew everywhere. By the end of the song, my arm was dripping wet, but I didn't care—we were having *fun*!

And then during the next song, Peter Tork came over to our side of the stage and bent down to shake hands with each of us wheelchair dwellers. As he made his way toward Tommy and me, I could see Tommy trying to raise his arm high enough to reach Peter's, but he just couldn't. So as soon as Peter (still cute as ever) stuck his hand in my direction, I grabbed it with both of mine and pulled him close enough for Tommy to envelop in a big bear hug.

Peter was a great sport, and I mean to tell you that was one Monkee who knew he'd been thoroughly hugged.

When the last train finally left for Clarksville, the lights came up and a white-haired couple appeared from the "regular" seats behind us. It was a good thing, too, because I didn't know how I was going to extricate my hand from Tommy's—he'd had a death grip on my blood-starved fingers during the last three songs. The woman—Tommy's mother—had tears in her eyes.

"Tommy doesn't get out much," she said, smiling at her boy, who kept his eyes glued to my face as if he were memorizing my features. "Most people are afraid to touch him, but you've been gracious enough to treat him like anyone else. I've never seen him so happy. He's always been a daydream believer, and now you're his homecoming queen. Thank you for giving him the best night of his life."

The best night of his life? I was stunned.

For weeks afterward I thought about what she'd said. I hadn't been trying to do anything good, nothing *gracious* at all. Yet the Lord used the unlikely combination of a skiing accident, a generous husband, a bubblegum concert, and a fraudulent handicapped gal to pour out His love on a very special young man.

Maybe that's what goodness is. . .nothing from within ourselves, but everything from God's orchestration. Perhaps goodness is not something we can manufacture by our own power but only channel from our heavenly Father. "No one is good but One, that is, God," Jesus reminded us in Matthew 19:17 (NKJV).

In the Spirit's fruit basket, goodness is the cantaloupe—sweet and juicy and bursting with the unique flavor of its Creator. God's flavor, His essence, *is* goodness. And the only way we can exude goodness in our lives is if He is dwelling within us.

You know, I've never been a beauty queen of any kind, but I have to tell you I'm moved beyond words to be Tommy's homecoming queen. It's a title I'll wear with honor until the day I go to live in my forever home with my Homecoming King.

*If truth is beauty, how come no one
has their hair done in the library?*
LILY TOMLIN

Taming the Beast

1. Why do you think goodness is included in the fruit of the Spirit?
2. If goodness can't be self-generated, what must we do to attain it?
3. Name a time when God orchestrated the seemingly unrelated events of your life to become someone's homecoming queen, even for a few moments. How did His goodness channel through you to touch his or her life?

CHAPTER 24
Silk Ribbons

(Faithfulness)

"I will take away your stubborn heart and give
you a new heart and a desire to be faithful."

EZEKIEL 36:26 CEV

Faithfulness is really a kind of fruit salad made up of all the other fruits
of the Spirit (love, joy, peace, patience, kindness, goodness, gentleness,
and self-control). When the menagerie of fruits are mixed together in
one bowl (person), a beautiful countenance and faithful lifestyle result.
Like sweet ambrosia!

By definition, to be faithful is to be steadfast in allegiance, to be
loyal above all else. . .in other words, *acting out* your relationship with
the Lord. Physically demonstrating where your heart lies.

Make no mistake, sister, your actions testify loud and clear to your
degree of faithfulness, whether you're aware of it or not. If you don't
think lifestyle faithfulness shows, you're dead wrong. People can spot
sincere faithfulness like a silk ribbon on a warthog.

While visiting a Russian Orthodox Church in Moscow several
years after the wall came down, my friend Don met with the rector
after Sunday services. When the rector mentioned that the average
attendance was eighty, Don was confused. "But there were more than
two hundred here this morning, how can that be?"

"We count differently, you and me," the rector replied with a kind
smile. "You see the tree, but I see the fruit. If I look at a man's life and

he's one quarter faithful, I count one quarter. If he is 50 percent faithful, I count half. For the teen who is here only because her mother made her come, I count zero. Only the truly faithful count as a complete *one*."

It makes me wonder what number Jesus counts when He looks at my life.

But you know what? It makes my hope soar when I see that even a prostitute scored a full point on the faithfulness scale in the Old Testament Faithfulness Hall of Fame found in Hebrews 11. Rahab the harlot was one of a handful of people lauded for their outstanding faithfulness despite trying circumstances (if you need an adrenaline boost, this is your go-to chapter!).

Remember Rahab's story? It's found in Joshua 2:1–21 and 6:22–25. She saved the lives of the two Israelite spies in the fortressed city of Jericho by hiding them and then helping them escape the bloodthirsty king's soldiers. All because she believed that God would empower their army to conquer her city. Because of her faith in the true almighty God, rather than the faux gods of her own people, Rahab and her family were spared when the walls came a'tumblin' down.

Rahab was the unlikeliest of heroes—a woman who sold her body to lusty men in dark shadows. Scum, we might say today. Yet she was the very person God chose to become a vital link in the lineage of King David, and later, Jesus Christ Himself. If a call girl can overcome her shady past and be extolled for her faithfulness, why can't we? Mother Teresa said, "Infinite possibilities are born of faith." Rahab is proof that God can—and will—use anyone with faith for His higher purposes. *Anyone.* How astoundingly freeing!

But it's important to note that Rahab didn't just skulk around, privately believing in God's power. She *acted* on her faith. She put her

feet where her faith was.

We have many modern-day role models of faithfulness, women who put their feet where their faith is. Among them are Ruth Graham, Corrie ten Boom, Joni Eareckson Tada. . .and Cookie Gray. "Um, who is that last one?" you might ask.

Cookie is a Faithfulness Hall of Famer from my little world. With humor and grace she's endured a lifetime of illness, surgeries, isolation, unmerited prejudice, and uphill climbing. *From her wheelchair.* She's a beautiful woman whose poise and radiant smile would never reveal the seventy years she's spent battling disability since contracting polio as a toddler. It was a personal milestone that Cookie, using crutches and leg braces, walked to the church altar as an eight-year-old to accept Christ as her personal Savior.

Since the day she turned her life over to Jesus, Cookie has depended on Him to carry her through life's hardships. Like when she got all the way through college with top grades only to be refused a teaching certificate solely because of her disabilities. And when she became a widowed mother at age forty.

"God sustained me through it all," Cookie says in her soft, confident voice. "I know exactly what 'pray without ceasing' means; my constant prayer has been 'Lord, help me through *this* day.'"

As director of the LifeCare Center in Brandon, Florida, since 1987, Cookie has taken very seriously her mission to strengthen households based on God's principles for building families. "I've been blessed with the gifts of discernment and a true love for people." That helps explain the phenomenal growth of the center from its meager beginning of one counselor to its current six-member staff, scores of volunteers, and up to four hundred client contacts each month.

"How," I asked, "do you do it? How do you remain faithful in the

down times? The parched desert times when your faith shrivels and you feel all alone?"

Cookie's answer, I believe, is insightful and applicable to all of us:

- Seek God as your source. Seek Him *first*; that will give you the courage to be bold and do whatever you need to do. "Seek first his kingdom and his righteousness, and all these things will be given to you as well" (Matthew 6:33 NIV).
- Use your gifts in His name. We're responsible to use our gifts, our abilities, and yes, our *disabilities* to draw focus to Him. Even a wheelchair can be His platform.
- Feed yourself daily. Listen to great teachers, read devotionals and Christian books, soak in faith-based music. Make yourself available to grow spiritually, emotionally, and mentally.
- Reach out through your smile. A warm smile draws people to you and gives them permission to be kind. It's the foundation for great relationships and carries enormous healing potential.
- Stay as beautiful as you can be, inside and outside. Keep yourself clean and neat, pleasant in appearance and attitude. People will respect you as much as you respect yourself. Never forget whom you represent.
- Talk yourself through difficulties. Everybody has daily aches and pains, and not just physically. Literally tell yourself you can overcome this obstacle, step by step—or wheel by wheel— and believe it.

Yep, I have no doubt Cookie counts as a complete *one* on God's faithfulness scale. She's been a personal inspiration to many people for decades.

Observing Cookie's perseverance and endurance reminds me that being faithful over a long period of time (like Noah building the ark month after month while his neighbors ridiculed him and rain was nowhere in sight) is harder than jumping out of the boat one time (as in Peter leaping out to walk to Jesus on the water in Matthew 14:29).

My brand of faithfulness tends to be boat-jumping as the occasion arises—more like clambering out of my kayak to wade in the shallows—rather than a lifestyle of hammering away at my ark under a cloudless sky.

But I want to become a dedicated ark-builder. . .to no longer count as just one half or even three quarters on that faithfulness scale. . .to put my feet where my faith is. How about you?

Faithful servants never retire. You can retire from your career,
but you will never retire from serving God.

RICK WARREN

Taming the Beast

1. Using the faithful-counting quotient of the Russian rector, what number do you think represents your degree of faithfulness?
2. Proverbs 3:3 instructs us, "Let love and faithfulness never leave you" (NIV). Why do you think this verse is important to remember?
3. Who is the Faithfulness Hall of Famer in your little world? What can you learn from this person's life to apply to your own?

Chapter 25
Lingering Fragrances

(Gentleness)

Cultivate inner beauty, the gentle,
gracious kind that God delights in.

1 Peter 3:4 msg

The score is tied at six games all in the third set. It's time to launch a tiebreaker; the first team to win seven points becomes the tennis match champion. I'm hyped, stoked, itching to *win*! My nerves tingle and bounce like electric Ping-Pong balls. *Let's go! Can't lose momentum! I got to move it, move it. . . .*

Pumped, I search for my laid-back partner, Lanie, who has moseyed on over onto another court to casually chat about a new restaurant in town.

Arrgh! Why can't she focus? Why isn't she as serious about this as I am?

At this point I should explain that this tennis partner is not one I've chosen; we were paired by our community league captain to keep the peace among the ten women on our team. (Any time you lump ten gals together for four months, you're at risk of fireworks!) She thought Lanie and I would get along because we were both Christians, even though we had completely opposite games.

We're an odd couple to be sure; I'm an aggressive slicer-dicer who plays to win the point quickly, and Lanie is what we call a defensive backboard—instead of putting the ball away, she hits everything back, invoking long rallies. I love overhead smashes; she avoids them. She lobs and lobs and lobs; I'd rather stick hot needles in my eye. Neither style is better or worse, just maddeningly different.

So the tiebreaker begins for Felix and Oscar. Our opponents win the first point up the middle, a hard passing shot betwixt Lanie and me. They win the second point down Lanie's sideline. They win the third point on an overhead smash from one of Lanie's too-short lobs. All the while my attitude is tanking fast. I'm actually starting to snort like an angry bull at a bullfight.

Not a pretty sight—or sound.

When we lose the fourth point (up the middle again), my inner beast erupts and I completely lose my cool. I proceed to skewer Lanie with my bloodied horns, using a barbed admonition to "At least stick your racket out now and then, will ya?" with all the sensitivity and gentleness of a charging bull.

I'm instantly sorry as I see Lanie's head droop and her shoulders slump. I know she's doing the best she can, but in the heat of battle, I lose vision of why I'm really out here. It's not to win at any cost. Not to morph into Maria Sharapova. In fact, it has nothing to do with tennis at all. I'm here to edify and uplift Lanie. That's what Papa God told me before our very first match, when I asked Him why in the world He put us together.

"Your purpose," He spoke to my heart, *"is not about you, it's about her."*

Okay, I blew it.

"Be humble and gentle. Be patient with each other, making allowance for each other's faults because of your love" (Ephesians 4:2 NLT). Gentle I ain't. But doggone it, I do want to be.

Can you identify with my angst? Many of us yearn to be gentle and patient and humble, but that blasted beast keeps getting in the way.

Gentleness is the delicate, fragrant mango in the fruit basket of the Spirit. There's no aroma quite like it. Gentleness is like a lovely scent that lingers behind us, a trace of God's exquisite fragrance in our own hearts that we leave in our wake, pointing others to Him.

We all know gentle, gracious people who do just that, don't we? Women whose intangible beauty glows from within. People who may not possess society's standards of physical beauty, but leave us basking in their elegant beauty nonetheless.

A perfect example is my friend Delia. I'm not using her real name because I know if I did, she'd die a thousand deaths when this book comes out (yes, she's *that* humble!). But everyone who knows her will recognize her immediately.

Delia, soft-spoken and gentle as a lamb, taught children's Sunday school in the same church I did several years ago; you can imagine our contrasting styles. While my technique of controlling a roomful of lively kids was to outscream them, Delia's was to whisper. No kidding! I would have never believed it if I hadn't seen it for myself. Time after time, Delia would turn a wild circus into a quiet, focused atmosphere by speaking confidentially in her lowest tones, as if sharing a special secret. The kids were mesmerized by her sweet, melodic voice and, without anyone telling them to, would quiet down in order to hear every word. She was beloved among the children because of her loving, gentle spirit and nonthreatening manner. Kind of like a female Mr. Rogers.

And you know the most amazing thing? Delia's gentleness truly did translate into outer beauty, just like it says in 1 Peter 3:4: "You should clothe yourselves. . .with the beauty that comes from within, the unfading beauty of a gentle and quiet spirit, which is so precious to God" (NLT). Precious to God and to those of us crazies needing a calming, steadying influence.

Delia's quite pretty, but people don't recall her physical appearance as much as they remember her inner beauty. They're two different things, you know. Delia always reminded me of a gardenia blossom—pure in radiant whiteness, intensely fragrant, and beautiful beyond compare; every heart she touched carried away the lingering scent of her heavenly Father's love.

That day on the tennis court, I reeked more of sour grapes than beautiful gardenias, or even refreshing mangos. But I really, *really* want to refill my atomizer with the lovely scent of Philippians 4:5: "Let your gentleness be evident to all" (NIV).

So how do I do that? How do I tenderize a tough, gristled slab of meat like myself into a filet mignon like Delia? Papa God gives a few gentle hints from His Word.

- "A gentle response defuses anger" (Proverbs 15:1 MSG). *I'm* responsible for what proceeds out of my mouth; no one *makes* me respond in anger or irritation. If I keep my prime directive front and center (like my goal to edify Lanie on the tennis court), it will be much easier to cage the raging beast and respond with gentleness.

- "Conduct yourselves in a manner worthy of the gospel of Christ" (Philippians 1:27 NASB). This would include empathizing with others. A good example is Jesus' gentle response when He cried with Mary and Martha in mourning their brother's death, although He knew Lazarus would be restored to life and health in a matter of hours. "Jesus wept" (John 11:35 NIV). One of the shortest but most powerful verses in the Bible. Jesus chose to tenderly enter their grief and feel their pain. We, too, should try to look beneath a surface of bad behavior and gently respond to the raw need hidden there. Empathy opens up a channel directly from the heart to the Holy Spirit.

- "If you are always biting and devouring one another, watch out! Beware of destroying one another" (Galatians 5:15 NLT). Our lack of gentleness is not benign; it can actually be destructive to the point of death. Not necessarily physical death but death of someone's self-esteem, her zest for life, her spirit. That's why it's important to cultivate this fruit of the Spirit, to spend time developing gentleness. To not give up when we blow it, like I did with my tennis partner.

- "A gentle tongue can break a bone" (Proverbs 25:15 NIV). Don't you *love* this verse? It makes me smile! I adore short, pithy scriptures—they're easy to memorize and always handy for everyday application. This one is truth with a zinger for competitive spirits like mine. Meditate on this verse for a day and you'll be amazed at the different ways it speaks to you!

- "Your gentleness has made me great" (Psalm 18:35 NKJV). Since God chose to create me with the natural gentleness of a typhoon, it's going to have to be *His* gentleness that transforms my inner beast and shines through me. That's the only greatness I'll ever achieve, not anything I do on my own. And I must remember to give Him the glory for each gentle victory!

Are you wondering how my tennis story ended? Well, we lost that match, but, praise God, I was able to win my personal beastie battle that day. The nasty barb that flew out of my mouth stunned me into silence for the rest of the tiebreaker, and when I got home, I called Lanie and profusely apologized. She is obviously further along on her 1 Peter 3:4 journey (earlier in this chapter) than I am and graciously forgave me.

Lanie and Delia both leave telltale scents of Christ's presence in their lives. Their lingering fragrance is my ultimate goal. I may go through a few dead skunks before I get there, but thankfully I know a great fumigator!

Nothing is so strong as gentleness, nothing so gentle as real strength.

SAINT FRANCIS DE SALES

Taming the Beast

1. How ripe is the fruit of gentleness in your spiritual basket? How strong is the lingering fragrance you leave behind?
2. Whom do you know that you would consider a truly gentle soul? What do you think is the key to his or her gentleness?
3. Which of the scriptures from my bouquet of gentle scriptural hints can you pluck and apply to your own journey toward gentleness?

Chapter 26
Melted Earrings

(Self-Control)

Keep your mouth shut, and you will stay out of trouble.

Proverbs 21:23 nlt

I staggered inside from the downpour and, through globs of hair hanging over my makeup-smeared face, I stared around the meeting room. Why couldn't they have arranged for me to park closer to the building in this storm? My best suit dripped onto my waterlogged shoes. I stood clutching the pathetic remnants of eighty dollars' worth of my newly released books I'd just spilled in a parking lot mud puddle, a pull-crate full of equipment, two tote bags of limp handouts, and my drenched laptop case, hoping against hope that it was waterproof.

This was definitely *not* worth the thirty-five dollars they were paying me.

Conversation tittered around me as if I were invisible instead of the guest speaker who'd driven 150 miles to be there. Nobody cared. Nobody even noticed. There was no table for my props and equipment, no screen for my PowerPoint, no. . .nothing.

Could I be in the wrong place?

The perfectly coiffed writing group coordinator who'd invited me finally tore herself away from her interchange with several other ladies, just long enough to introduce herself and inform me that the power strip I'd requested *three weeks before* was unavailable for my PowerPoint presentation so I'd just have to make do without it. Oh,

and by the way, she mentioned as an afterthought, she'd been too busy to get the workshop advertisement out on time so there probably wouldn't be much of a turnout. Then, without further ado, she turned back to her previous conversation.

What? No PowerPoint? You've got to be kidding! I wanted to holler. *That's my whole program. What do you expect me to do for two hours without it? Strip to my undies and belly dance?*

Swallowing hard, I walked to a window and stared out at the rain, not really seeing it. I could feel that ravenous inner beast clawing his way up my esophagus, gathering venom to spew everywhere as he emerged to rip and rant and plunder.

Okay, time out. What would you have done at this point in this true scenario? Besides wet your pants? (Mine were already wet from the rain, so it didn't matter!)

If you said, "I'd blast the sorry sucker till her earrings melted," then you're in the right chapter, girlfriend. That's exactly how I felt. But, contrary to every screaming fiber within me, by the grace of God, that's *not* what I did. Stay tuned for the thrilling finale.

Self-control is the prune of the Spirit; *not* the fruit you savor but the one vital for moving things along smoothly. (If you've ever drunk prune juice, you know what I mean!) It's the fruit you gulp down and try not to choke on.

I think it's no coincidence that self-control is listed just behind gentleness in Galatians 5; they sprout from the same vine. You need to ingest the first in order to digest the second.

Did you know that it's not wrong to be angry? Nope, not according to Ephesians 4:26–27: "Go ahead and be angry. You do well to be angry—but don't use your anger as fuel for revenge. And don't stay angry. Don't go to bed angry. Don't give the Devil that kind of

foothold in your life" (MSG).

Our God is a passionate God—He feels things. And He feels them strongly. We are made in His image, so we must never deny our feelings. We were created to feel. The only people who don't feel anger or resentment or jealousy are dead people. But after we passionately feel, we need to bring those emotions under Christ's submission and then react accordingly.

Regardless of what *The Sopranos* or *Fight Club*s of this world tell us, it's not wimpy or weak to stifle that scream or swallow that snippy retort that seemingly loads itself in your cannon, all ready to fire. Self-control is courage fueled by integrity and supernatural power. It's something the average Jane doesn't have; it is possessed only by those willing to step back from the firing line and hand over the lit match. "God's Spirit doesn't make cowards out of us. The Spirit gives us power, love, and self-control" (2 Timothy 1:7 CEV).

Did you catch that? *The Spirit gives us self-control.* That's where our best reactions come from—not our worst or even our natural reactions. Those are directly from the horse's mouth—or rather her patootie.

Our *best* reactions come from the Spirit who lives within us but sometimes gets buried beneath smothering piles of self: self-gratification, self-esteem issues, self-sufficiency. We forget how much we need Him until our cannon misfires a few times or we blow the head off an innocent bystander.

You know, sister, to exert self-control, we just need to barf. That's right, B-A-R-F! (Not very eloquent, I'm afraid, but I need tools that are short, direct, and work!)

- **B**ack off. Literally step back, walk away, or turn your back on the source of your anger. Withdraw to gain a new perspective. Take a deep breath. Ask the Spirit to calm you down and take over you.

- **A**dmit *why* you're upset. Give it a name: "Lord, I'm. . .furious, hurt, insulted, jealous, offended, irate, taken advantage of, envious. . . " Be as specific as you can. Identifying it is the first step in dealing with it.

- **R**edirect your emotions. Remember who is *really* responsible for eliciting the tempest within you—it's not the person(s) who offended you; it's the dude you don't see, the evil, chuckling one with the proverbial pitchfork stuck in your back. Direct your anger toward the Devil with a physical, symbolic act: Point toward the floor, raise a clenched fist, close your eyes, and shake your head—do something to signify that Satan is the mastermind. Now let Jesus deal with *him*. The creep can't win.

- **F**orgive your offender and forgive yourself. It's the only way to find peace. Grudges corrode your soul. Ask God to let you see your offender through His eyes—it makes a *big* difference. Forgiveness may not happen right away; depending on the depth of the offense, it may take a while. That's okay. Just begin the process now by speaking civilly, calmly, and respectfully. You'll have nothing to regret later.

So back to my workshop fiasco. . .here's how it played out when I BARFed.

You already know what I wanted to do, but you may not realize how badly I wanted to do it. *Real* bad. My blood was boiling. But instead I walked over to the window (backed off), took a deep breath, and shot off a prayer for help.

"Lord," I prayed, "I feel disrespected, unappreciated, and mad as a wet hen. In fact, I wish I *were* a wet hen. I want to peck the eyes out

of that woman who is treating me like barnyard crud on the bottom of her fancy Italian shoe" (admitted how I felt).

I gripped the windowsill until my knuckles were white, taking deep cleansing breaths all the while. When my blood pressure began to normalize, I slowly banged my fists on top of each other three times in my symbolic nail-Satan-in-his-coffin, cool-down gesture (redirected emotions).

"Papa God," I whispered, "help me forgive her. She's probably had a lousy, rotten, stinking day and her Victoria's Secret panties are giving her a wedgie. Maybe she was too busy to prepare for my workshop because her dog died."

I gotta tell you, this deceased dog thought always softens up the hard knot inside like nothing else. Try it! (Forgive.)

Then I dragged a table to the front of the room and began unloading my stuff. Several people came to my aid, including the coordinator. She actually turned out to be a nice person and raved about my books. I was glad I hadn't melted her earrings.

Maybe you're not so hot at this self-control thing. I'm not, either, but with the Holy Spirit's help and a little BARFing, I think I'm getting better. I don't fly apart as much as I used to, which is a major accomplishment. "If you fall to pieces in a crisis, there wasn't much to you in the first place" (Proverbs 24:10 MSG).

And happily, I haven't had to deal with wet pants lately. . .from any source.

*You must believe there is such a thing
as self-control before you can use it.*

UNKNOWN

Taming the Beast

1. Philippians 2:14 advises us to "Do everything without grumbling or arguing" (CEV). How does exerting self-control fit with this scripture?
2. When was the last time your reaction to a situation blew completely out of control? How did you handle it?
3. So the next time you're mad enough to barf, do it! Review what BARF stands for: back off, admit, redirect, forgive.

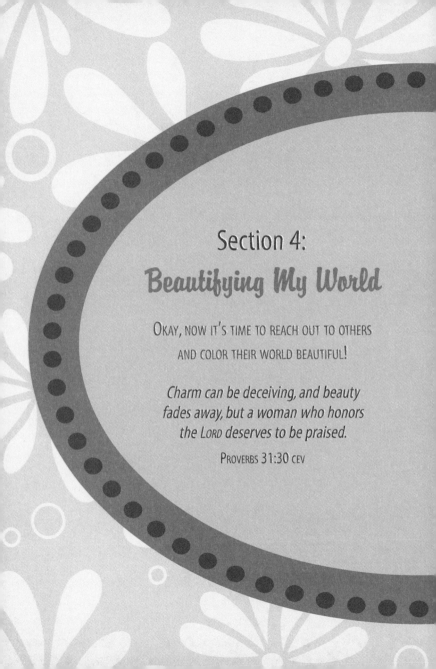

Section 4:

Beautifying My World

OKAY, NOW IT'S TIME TO REACH OUT TO OTHERS
AND COLOR THEIR WORLD BEAUTIFUL!

*Charm can be deceiving, and beauty
fades away, but a woman who honors
the Lord deserves to be praised.*

PROVERBS 31:30 CEV

Chapter 27
Boogies and Bosoms

(Friendship)

If you fall, your friend can help you up. But if you fall
without having a friend nearby, you are really in trouble.

ECCLESIASTES 4:10 CEV

Sweat stung my eyes, and steel butterflies ricocheted in my belly. My friend and tennis partner that season, Trina, had just rocketed a forehand shot down the line to tie the game score in the second set, 5 to 5. It was now my serve. The pressure was immense. We both knew our collective fate in the match depended on this game.

As I grabbed my towel from my tennis bag, Trina jogged over to join me.

"How should we play this?" I asked, turning my back to our opponents to keep our strategy secret. This was sobering stuff. We'd never been so close to beating this team before. My nerves began rattling louder than my knocking knees.

Handing me a tennis ball, Trina eyed me closely. Suddenly, the corners of her mouth twitched as if she was fighting a smile. And was that a twinkle in her eye?

Had to be my imagination. Although we loved to laugh together, there was nothing funny about this situation. We had our game faces on. Serious tactical discussion was essential if we had a prayer of winning.

I had just launched into a strategic game plan utilizing my tricky slice serve and Trina's Linda Ronstadt baseline blast, affectionately known as her "Blue Bayou" shot (blew-by-you—get it?), when Trina interrupted.

"Boogie at three o'clock."

"Wh–what?" I asked, dumbfounded.

"You know, three o'clock; if your face is a clock, your bangs are at twelve, your chin is at six—"

"What in heaven's name are you talking about? This is the most stressful match of the year and you're spouting gibberish?"

A toothy smile creased her sweat-glistened face from ear to ear. "You've got a boogie hanging out of your left nostril, girlfriend. It's a squishy one, too. Why don't you add a little lubrication to that slice of yours and serve up a boogie ball?"

Girlfriends. What would we do without 'em? They're our link to levity when reality becomes too intense, our safety nets when we're free falling, the purveyors of painful truth who break it to us ever so gently and then share our pain. They're the distributors of grace when we're fragile, tears when we're broken, and warm hugs to help fit the pieces back together.

Girlfriends are the rare finds who hear the songs down deep in our souls and care enough to sing a duet when we can't manage a solo.

Everyone needs a soul sister, a kindred spirit who offers unconditional love and acceptance. Someone who believes we *can* be beautiful and overlooks our inner beast when it takes a bite out of her booty. A safe place where we can store our secrets and be sure they won't leak. Aristotle said, "The antidote for fifty enemies is one friend."

Anne of Green Gables was right about girls needing bosom friends, someone who *understands* intimately, someone whom we hold close to our hearts, knowing she reciprocates. Take Jan, for example. She's been my best friend since the sixth grade. We've been bosom buddies since, well, since we got bosoms. (Nothing's wrong with the special men in our lives, of course, but their bosoms just aren't the same.) I can tell Jan anything and know she won't judge. She'll always look for the faintest spark of beauty in me and fan it to flames.

Some ladies tell me they find it hard to make friends, but I've found a trick. I call it my "friendly lid theorem" (another Coty near-fact of science). Here it is: People who wear kicky hats make more friends! I ain't funnin' ya! It's true! Men have known this conversation-starting secret for years: wear a logo baseball cap and every other man you encounter will comment.

The concept works for women, too, only with adorable headwear. I do it all the time, and I tell you, it works. In fact, I had a delightful conversation with another "hat girl" just yesterday as we—total strangers enjoying fedora fellowship—tried on hats together in a department store. She wholeheartedly agreed with my friendly lid theorem and added, "I think others smile because they secretly wish they were wearing one, too!"

Yep, girlfriends can be found anywhere, sometimes in the oddest places.

In my job as an occupational therapist, a charming sixty-something-year-old patient arrived for therapy one day, arm in arm with a snowy-haired friend. She introduced me to her "wife-in-law."

"Um, I'm not sure I understand that relationship," I responded as the two ladies giggled like teenage BFFs.

"After my divorce, she married my ex-husband," my patient explained. "Then he died and we became best friends." Oookay. You just never know where you'll find a soul sister!

Girlfriends don't necessarily have *everything* in common. One of the gals on my tennis team is a self-avowed atheist and is as politically liberal as I am conservative. We differ on every social and theological issue. But she faithfully shows up at my Christian bookstore signings, buying my books for her "religious" mother-in-law just to support me. She may not understand or even agree with my views, but her loyalty and thoughtfulness supersede all boundaries. I feel honored to call her my friend.

Friendship doesn't recognize age. One of the most beloved passages in the Bible is between Ruth and her mother-in-law, Naomi. Although of different generations, both women have suffered the devastating losses of their husbands and Naomi has decided to return to her homeland. With a breaking heart, she urges Ruth to stay in her own country with her parents and support system. Through hot tears, Ruth whispers those heart-stirring words that are now repeated as wedding vows: "Where you go, I will go, and where you lodge, I will lodge. Your people shall be my people, and your God, my God" (Ruth 1:16 NASB).

How revealing that this beautiful declaration of allegiance between friends is regarded as the foundation for loyalty in marriage. Friendship is not to be taken lightly. God views true friendship as a relationship with bonds as deep and strong and sacred as those between a husband and wife. That means friendship, like marriage, requires maintenance and attention, including a little TLC (tender loving care) and gentle patching up when feelings inevitably get scraped or bruised.

"A friend loves at all times" (Proverbs 17:17 NASB). We can tell a bosom friend by her degree of blindness when looking at our faults. And we know that our bosom friend will always be there for us—through bloated and svelte, sweet and grumpy, thoughtful and insensitive, tissues and boogies.

*Friendship isn't a big thing—
it's a million little things.*

UNKNOWN

Taming the Beast

1. So which girlfriend is *your* safety net? Your soul sister whom you can't imagine living without? Have you told her so lately? Go on— give her a liver-squeezing hug and make her wonder what you've been sniffing.

2. Who is your most unlikely friend? You know, the one you really *shouldn't* click with in theory but do in an amazing way? What brought you two together?

3. Do you have any relationships with friends in your past or present that may need a little TLC? What's stopping you? Take the first step and give her a call.

CHAPTER 28
Perky Slipcovers

(Forgiveness)

"When you are praying, first forgive anyone you are holding a grudge
against, so that your Father in heaven will forgive your sins, too."

MARK 11:25–26 NLT

The dark, handsome Spanish swashbuckler and the dashing blond
masked man engage in a mighty swordfight, but only after the Spaniard
has spilled his sad story of witnessing his beloved father's death at the
hands of the mysterious six-fingered man. He has spent his entire life
seeking revenge for his father's murder.

The two eventually team up with a gentle giant for rollicking
adventures revolving around the kidnapping of a beautiful princess.
The courageous buccaneer finally faces his long-sought-after foe and
we watch in edge-of-the-chair suspense as the six-fingered man first
jams his blade into the Spaniard's left, then his right shoulder.

Oh no! All is lost. No revenge tonight.

But wait! Suddenly our hero is infused with renewed strength and
screams, "My name is Inigo Montoya. You *keeled* my father; prepare to
die!" And we find ourselves cheering as he plunges his sword into the
evil, deserves-to-die villain.

Sound familiar? If you're a fan of *The Princess Bride*, you'll recognize
one of the most famous revenge scenes in modern cinema. Ah, revenge
is sweet, isn't it?

Isn't it?

I have to admit, in Inigo's fictional case, it most certainly feels like it. But what about real life? A *believer's* real life?

God actually has a different take on revenge. "Never pay back evil with more evil. . . . Dear friends, never take revenge. Leave that to the righteous anger of God. For the Scriptures say, 'I will take revenge; I will pay them back,' says the Lord" (Romans 12:17, 19 NLT).

"What? We shouldn't seek revenge?" we cry in outrage! "C'mon— it's only fair! What else can possibly satisfy that burning desire for justice in the depths of our being?"

Forgiveness. Yes, ma'am, that's right.

But forgiveness doesn't come naturally in our revenge-glorified world. Because forgiveness is often impossible without the Holy Spirit's intervention, we feed off the power of one-upping someone who has wronged us. Forgiving and accepting forgiveness are unique qualities in today's society.

There's an *otherworldly* tenderness inherent to forgiveness that flies in the face of the Rambos, Terminators, and Godfathers of our day. We're drawn to revenge-seekers because we secretly wish we could dominate our enemies, too. We admire avengers, popularize them, and even wear their pictures on our T-shirts.

Could that be part of the reason why we—who desire to be like Christ more than anything else—find it so hard to forgive?

Probably. But I think it's mostly because we just plain don't feel like it.

In the midst of our get-you-back frenzies, it's hard to remember that how we *feel* has nothing to do with forgiveness. We forgive as an act of the will, because God commands us to, not because of feelings. If we wait to feel like it, we'll never forgive anybody.

The act of forgiveness enables God to perform a mysterious

and profound work of grace in us. The healing process begins—first inwardly, in our own hearts, then outwardly—in the broken relationship with our offenders. As we release others from the hurt they've caused us, our own pain and bitterness are miraculously (and I use this term intentionally) released. Anger stops holding us prisoner. Resentment no longer eats away at our intimacy with God.

The gnawing beast within is muzzled.

My friend Karen, who has struggled with the bondage of unforgiveness in her family for decades, says, "Forgiveness is a powerful thing. We desperately need it and should freely give it."

But forgiving someone is only half the equation. Being forgiven when we've wronged others is crucial—not only for our personal peace of mind, but to keep from curling up in a ball and withering away from demoralizing remorse. We do and say so many hurtful things, how can we *not* be immobilized by guilt?

My friend Cherylyn told me a chilling story that illustrated this perfectly.

On the day of Cherylyn's graduation from high school, the seniors only had to show up that night for the ceremony, so she was home alone reveling in her freedom while her parents were at work. On a whim, she decided to fry up some deviled crab cakes for lunch. Ignoring the strong fumes from the adhesive her mom had just used to wallpaper the kitchen, Cherylyn heated up Crisco on the stove then dropped a couple frozen crab cakes into the hot grease.

As soon as the icy cakes hit the scalding pan, sparks flew as if she'd sprinkled gasoline on a lit burner. Fed by flammable adhesive fumes, flames erupted, instantly igniting the wallpaper behind the stove in one huge *whish*, and spread throughout the small kitchen like, well, wildfire. Cherylyn panicked as black soot shot everywhere and thick,

acrid smoke began to penetrate every corner of the house. All she could do was grab the dog and run, barely making it to the door before passing out. A neighbor pulled her away from the inferno and together they helplessly watched much of Cherylyn's house go up in flames.

When her horrified parents arrived, her mother rushed up to Cherylyn, crying, "Are you all right?" Her father's first reaction was to shake his head in disbelief and utter, "How could you do this?"

The graduation ceremony that night went on as planned, but Cherylyn's heart was weighted with grief. She just wanted to run away and hide. The awards she received did little to dent the shame she felt for causing her beloved father's anger and condemnation. She could feel the rift in their relationship down to her bone marrow. She was completely and utterly miserable and felt unworthy to be called his daughter.

Then something happened that changed everything. As Cherylyn tearfully walked across the stage to receive her diploma, a deep voice resonated through the packed auditorium. "That's my baby girl!" Cherylyn turned to see the lone figure of her dad among the sea of onlookers, his face glowing with pride.

She was forgiven! Cherylyn knew she didn't deserve it; she'd done nothing to earn it, yet there it was in all its awesome, freeing glory; forgiveness redeemed her night, her heart, her *life*.

It's true that we can't *make* other people forgive us. But we can sure ask them to. That's all Papa God wants us to do. . .ask. That, of course, requires swallowing our egos and chewing a little self-importance gristle. But temporary pride indigestion is well worth getting rid of stinking, slimy leftover guilt and self-loathing that blotches our inner beauty, making us perceive ourselves as tainted. Dirty. Ugly.

And *nobody* wants to feel ugly.

A few years ago, I needed a couch that would double as a guest bed for my home office. I didn't want to spend a lot of money on something few people would ever see, so I was tickled pink when someone said she had a sleeper sofa she'd give me.

Give is good! I like *give*!

It wasn't until after we'd gone to all the backbreaking labor to transfer this heavy monstrosity to my tiny office that I really looked at it for the first time. It was ugly. No way around it; ugly with a capital *U*. Although quite comfortable, the couch was old and the dated fabric was worn transparent in places. For some reason, it reminded me of an aging hippopotamus.

So I frowned at the hideous hippo in my office for two weeks before an idea hit me. I found the perfect answer online. Within ten days, that pathetic old couch had been given new life with a cute denim slipcover and throw pillows to match my denim-and-sunflower office motif. The whole room perked up!

Forgiveness is the slipcover for the soul. We're not defined by our mistakes; we're recovered and remodeled by forgiveness. We're made new and perky and beautiful! No one need ever remember the ugliness underneath—God guarantees us that He won't! "As far as the east is from the west, so far has he removed our transgressions from us" (Psalm 103:12 NIV).

So what do you think, sister? Does the stained couch of your life need a jazzy new slipcover? I hear the Divine Forgiveness Boutique is running a special!

Forgiveness is the gift I give to myself. . .
sometimes that's the hardest person to forgive!
SANDRA EDWARDS HAZEN

Taming the Beast

1. Is there a six-fingered man in your life? Someone who deserves to die (figuratively, of course) or at least suffer a little?
2. Are you ready to make the decision to forgive? Remember, it's a matter of the will, not feelings.
3. Is there someone whom you need to ask for forgiveness? Are you brave enough to lift that question to Papa God in prayer and quietly listen for His answer?

CHAPTER 29

Tempted by the Dark Side: Chocolate

(Transcending Barriers)

Seize life! Eat bread with gusto, drink wine with a robust heart.
Oh yes—God takes pleasure in your pleasure!

ECCLESIASTES 9:7 MSG

The young Hindu woman kept her eyes downcast as she sat at the narrow table in my physical therapy clinic. I had been treating Uma's painful elbow tendonitis for two weeks and hadn't been able to break through the puzzling, invisible barrier between us.

For over thirty years, I've viewed my patients as my ministry and continually pray for their spiritual well-being as I labor toward their physical health. The Lord blessed me with the gift of acceptance, and through my therapy work I've become friends with people of all cultures and faiths, as well as pimps, drug dealers, prostitutes, and criminals (some in orange jumpsuits and handcuffs and others not so obvious).

As with all my patients, I'd been trying to extend Papa God's love to Uma, but my efforts had bounced off a stone wall.

Uma was a lovely, petite Indian woman in her thirties with smooth, mocha skin and guarded ebony eyes. Although she dressed in beautiful saris and matching head scarves fashioned from exquisite fabrics, her cheerless demeanor and defeated body language suggested depression. I just couldn't seem to make an emotional connection to let her know that I cared.

Then one day Uma arrived for therapy, swathed from head to toe in fine cream-colored material covered with thin brown stripes. With my usual impulsive leap of tongue before brain, I gushed, "Oh my goodness, you look like a giant Hershey's Hug!"

By the sudden grin and sparkle in her eye, I knew we'd found common ground at last! I unearthed my secret stash of chocolates and poured them out on the table before her. It was the first time I'd seen her smile.

During the following weeks, surrounded by growing piles of foil wrappers as we worked, Uma gradually opened up. Her husband's job was out of state and he was only able to come home one weekend a month, leaving her functioning as a single parent for their two children. Having no family or close friends in the area, she felt overwhelmed and lonely.

Surprised and obviously moved when I mentioned that I'd been praying for her, Uma confessed that she had begun to question tenets of the faith into which she'd been born and expressed an interest in learning more about Christianity.

What a golden opportunity to share the hope and joy of my Jesus!

Since my book *Mom NEEDS Chocolate* hadn't been written yet (and indeed this incident with Uma was a major motivator for the book's inception as a border-transcending, women's faith-sharing instrument!), I ran out and purchased a copy of Karen Scalf Linamen's classic, *Just Hand over the Chocolate and No One Will Get Hurt.* Presenting this seeker-friendly book to Uma on her last therapy appointment, along with a warm hug (real, not chocolate), my phone number, and a box of Ferrero Rocher, I assured her that she would continue to be in my heart and prayers.

Who would have ever considered chocolate an evangelism tool? Come to think of it, I suspect our Master Designer did when He created most women the world over with a craving for that sweet, creamy, luscious stuff. It's a common denominator, the silk thread that connects us at a deeper level. A visceral level. A happy tummy level. After all, it's common knowledge that the way to a girl's heart is through her Ghirardelli!

And it's practically guilt-free! In a German study following almost twenty thousand people for eight years, research published in the *European Heart Journal* reported that those consuming the equivalent of one dark chocolate square daily (about six grams) had a 39 percent lower risk of heart attack or stroke. A great big *yay* for those flavanols in dark chocolate that widen blood vessels and lower blood pressure!

Believe it or not, since I lost forty pounds three years ago, I've not missed my chocolate fix one single day. The key, I've found, is to stick to my quota: eat four squares, not four bars; two Oreos (reduced fat) instead of two bags. It's amazing how even a small taste will satisfy that choco-craving.

Papa God thought of everything!

The problem is, of course, keeping our dosage high enough for palatal satisfaction and low enough to avoid rib rolls and thigh-u-lite. Or those wicked derriere dimples. Hey, if it weren't for the evidence of all those medicinal mocha lattes with our girlfriends, we'd be portraits of health and happiness!

In fact, I stumbled across a research study concluding something we girls already know—that weight and eating habits are influenced by our friends. We tend to embrace the good (and bad) habits of our peeps. So if we hang out with Frappuccino addicts, we're likely to join the ranks. And vice versa.

So how can we apply our affinity for choco-scarfing with friends to spread the joy and hope of Christ? I have a suggestion.

After the release of *Mom NEEDS Chocolate*, I began having Choc-OUT parties. The hour-long parties are hosted in private homes, in which the hostess invites her friends, neighbors, and coworkers for a hilarious girls night out during which we sample chocolate (everyone brings their fave chocolate dessert to share). We also play chocolate games, like seeing who can be the first to peel and consume five Hershey's Kisses with their hands encased in thick wool socks. Then we sing into hairbrushes along to a hysterical chocolate parody of Kelly Clarkson's "Because of You," adapted by Jim McKenzie on YouTube under the title "Because of You (Chocolate)" with lyrics like:

> *Because of you, I never stray too far from the ice box.*
> *Because of you, I learn to make a mudslide when my feelings hurt;*
> *Because of you, I find that I must eat not only you but everything around me.*
> *Because of yooou. . .I am alive!*

And then when giggles have loosened tight tongues and spirits have bonded, we go a little deeper and share from our hearts how Jesus is as satisfying, necessary, and *real* in our lives as the Peterbrooke confection in our hands. We keep conversation light as we touch on our favorite scriptures or maybe offbeat food-related verses like the Ecclesiastes 9:7 at the beginning of this chapter; or Genesis 27:4: "Prepare me the kind of tasty food I like and bring it to me to eat, so that I may give you my blessing before I die" (NIV); or Deuteronomy 8:10: "When you have eaten and are satisfied, praise the LORD your

God for the good land he has given you" (NIV). Another is Philippians 3:19: "Easy street is a dead-end street. Those who live there make their bellies their gods; belches are their praise; all they can think of is their appetites" (MSG).

Then we close in prayer for each other's needs.

I've been amazed with the popularity of these casual choco-themed chick-chats and encourage you to consider inviting a group of your girlfriends over to Choc-OUT. It's a great way to reach out to believers and nonbelievers alike. Follow any format you like; Google chocolate games or songs, or create your own. Just plan on laughing loud and long, releasing tension, looking God-ward, rejuvenating spirits, and chillin' like only girlfriends can.

And you never know—some nice Hindu gal might just show up dressed like a Hershey's Hug!

> *What you see before you, my friend,*
> *is the result of a lifetime of chocolate.*
> KATHARINE HEPBURN

Taming the Beast

1. Are you, too, a choco-athlete? (I prefer this title over chocoholic.) Be honest now: do you struggle with obsession over chocolate, food, exercise, clothes, or any other *thing* that takes your focus off Christ?

2. Do you feel that your eating habits are influenced by the company you keep? Is this a good or a bad thing for you?

3. Have you ever considered using chocolate to reach out and touch someone in Christ's name? Think for a moment of a friend or even casual acquaintance who might benefit from a little chocolaty love gift from you today.

CHAPTER 30
The Weirdness That Binds

(Marriage)

Relish life with the spouse you love each
and every day of your precarious life.
Each day is God's gift. . . . Make the most of each one!

ECCLESIASTES 9:9 MSG

While teaching a young writers' workshop at a local high school, I overheard an enlightening conversation in the crowded teachers' lounge. One of the more venerable (read: silver-haired) teachers mentioned that she and her husband were celebrating their thirtieth wedding anniversary. After marinating on that thought for a long moment, a twentysomething coworker shook her head and asked, "How do you do that? How do you *like* somebody for thirty years?"

With a wink and wisdom born of a thousand makeup kisses, the woman replied, "Well, you may not. . .you may only like them for fifteen years, but you love them for thirty."

After a wave of gentle laughter rolled through the room, she explained further, "The longer you're married, you and your husband grow weird in the same way—a way nobody else understands. It's that weirdness that binds you together."

I'd never heard it described quite that way, but the truth resonated with me. Weird isn't always bad. Weird can be good. Weird is often why we fall in love over and over again—with the same person. Weird is superglue in a relationship.

Take my husband's weirdness, for example. (I, of course, have no weirdness of my own to report.) Now I'm the first to sing Chuck's praises as a true partner in knocking off household chores. In this respect he is quite normal—no, *better* than normal. He vacuums, scrubs sinks, makes beds, washes dishes. Lots and lots of dishes. Some of which land in the dishwasher but most he stacks in the dish drainer. And this is where the weird comes in. Trust me when I say I use the word *stacks* loosely. It's more like heaps. Piles on. Overloads.

What is it with men and competition? It's like a contest with him, a world championship to see how many plates, glasses, pots, and pans he can amass into a monstrous lurching mountain before the whole thing avalanches.

But does that hinder the game in any way? Nooo. He just keeps piling more on, meal after meal, day after day, excitement lighting his eyes when he climbs the stepladder to balance a crystal goblet atop a particularly colossal accumulation.

It used to really tick me off, this Mount Everest obsession of his. At first I'd sweetly point out that although he was oh, so very wonderful to wash the dishes, it would be even more helpful if he put them away. No dice. I progressed to unsuccessful grousing, complaining, and nagging. Then resentment and seething. *How does he think they're going to get into the cupboard—the dish fairy? Don't I have enough to do? Why does he have to play with everything? Who's going to clean up his mistakes?*

My tiny seed of anger sprouted into Jack's sky-high beanstalk.

And then one day nothing changed, but everything changed. My dear friend Rita lost her husband to cancer at age fifty-seven. As I stood in my kitchen, weeping with her on the phone, my eyes rested on that ridiculous mound of kitchenware in the dish drainer. Somehow this time it didn't needle me. I knew Rita would give anything to have

her husband's weird, maddening, endearing habits back for just one minute.

Inside me, something hard broke into a hundred little pieces.

And from that moment on, although the looming precipice threatening to bury the kitchen didn't change, my perspective did. I was able to release my annoyance. Let it go. To my amazement, I even smiled occasionally at Mount Saint Chuck.

Sound familiar? Do you struggle with some irritating little habit—or two, or six—of your husband's? It's okay to admit it—we all have those marital pet peeves that get under our skin. But let me share something that might help you understand your man's weirdness a little better.

We've all been indoctrinated into the witchy, wacky world of PMS, right? (That's "premenstrual syndrome," not "pretending Mom's sane.") Well, did you know there's such a thing as *male* PMS? Scientists call it irritable male syndrome (IMS), and it can really truly alter your man's personality. Researchers have discovered that up to 30 percent of men experience hormonal cycles strong enough to impact their temperaments, but it's more on a daily basis than monthly like ours. When testosterone levels dip (more often in the afternoon), so does your guy's mood; when it spikes (usually morning), aggression can morph him into the Hulk (minus the gangrene motif).[15]

Hmm. I wonder if guys have cravings and cramps, too. That could explain the Cadbury bar missing from my stash.

And males even experience a type of midlife menopause, as well; it's called *andropause*. While our estrogen is evacuating, their testosterone is busy jumping ship, too. Maybe that's the real reason for the red Ferrari and toupee!

Even with all the understanding in the world, we women will still

encounter some emotional gaps in our marriage. That's because we're married to *men*. Please don't misunderstand—I'm not male-bashing, just recognizing that our Creator wired us so that we're from different emotional planets and our spaceships travel in different orbits.

The thing is, we can't let those emotional gaps widen to the point that they form unbridgeable chasms, splitting asunder that sacred union we promised to cherish and protect until death do us part.

Some of my single friends are positive that one is the loneliest number. But when I allow those gaps to become chasms in my marriage, isolating each of us into our separate little worlds, I believe there is no lonelier number than a half. . .my half without his half that together makes us a whole.

Let me illustrate how those gaps-turned-chasms can start out innocently.

I'm a morning person in the worst way, meaning the rooster in my head crows at 5 a.m. Yes, it's a curse, but I've learned to use it to my advantage and have become extremely productive during the dark hours before dawn when everyone else is enjoying their final snooze. Anyway, because of my early rising, I have to be in bed by 10 p.m. in order to fall asleep by 11 (relaxing is a challenge for me) or I'm a useless zombie the next day.

Chuck, however, is a night person. He thinks nothing of working until the wee hours and rarely turns the light off before 2 a.m. You can imagine how this could be a problem for us.

During our first decades of marriage, Chuck simply sequestered himself in his home office while I trotted off to bed. But I began protesting that this just wasn't right. I'd bought into the fairy tale that married people were supposed to cuddle, kiss good night, and roll over into blissful sleep together. So I harped at Chuck until he changed his

wicked ways and dragged his reluctant keister into bed with me at ten o'clock.

After many restless nights (for both of us), he started bringing his laptop into bed, tapping away at those confounded keys. The bright screen made me feel as if I were starring in a Broadway production. I tried earplugs, eye patches, even sleeping with my pillow over my head (which is murder during hot flashes, believe you me).

Nothing worked.

So we began piling bolsters, quilts, and throw pillows between us like a miniature wall of China, higher and higher to block out light, sound, and all other vestiges of humanity. By this time, because each of us was so vexed that the other wouldn't compromise, neither of our stubborn inner ogres would concede that this wasn't a good solution.

The Great Wall of Coty only succeeded in blocking out intimacy—emotionally *and* physically—between us. But would you believe we obstinately continued this way for three years? *Three years!*

Finally, with our relationship teetering on emotional estrangement, I stumbled across 1 Corinthians 14:1: "Go after a life of love as if your life depended on it—because it does" (MSG). *Go after*, I heard Paul implore, as in *pursue*. Chase. Be proactive. Make it happen. Because if you don't, you'll miss out on love altogether. And, Debbie, you *need* love. Why, your very life depends on it.

I was tired of waiting for the gap to magically to fill in, for some solution to present itself that would rekindle the closeness, the intimacy, the passion we'd let lapse. I was tired of my husband being merely a roommate, a good friend with whom I shared dinner, kids, an occasional romp in the hay, but little emotional intimacy.

Enough already!

So in a fit of determination one night, I slugged my inner ogre in

the jaw, marched into the bedroom, and tore down the Great Wall of Coty. I'll never forget Chuck's surprised but pleased response when he came in, took one look at our bare bed, and heard me announce emphatically, "No more walls!"

The dear man put away his laptop, crawled in beside me, and gave me his undivided attention. There were no barriers between us, only vulnerable smiles and tentatively extended hands. We were ready to start building the bridge over that chasm we'd dug one plank at a time.

If you're straddling a relationship chasm right now, take heart, sister—it *can* be bridged. You *can* make it happen (remember 1 Corinthians 14:1!). . .with a little determination, creativity, and a *lot* of weirdness superglue!

> *Don't marry the person you think you can live with;*
> *marry only the individual you think you can't live without.*
> DR. JAMES DOBSON

Taming the Beast

1. What about you? What's your own peculiar brand of marital weirdness? Is it drawing you closer together or driving you apart?

2. The Lord's *best* remedy for loneliness is recorded in Psalm 68:6: "God sets the lonely in families" (NIV). Why do you think this is true?

3. In your marriage, are there any gaps at risk of turning into bottomless chasms? What bridge-building steps can you pursue? Remember, you *need* love; your very life depends on it!

CHAPTER 31
Garden Party

(Creating a Legacy)

You must be very careful not to forget the things you
have seen God do for you. Keep reminding yourselves,
and tell your children and grandchildren as well.

DEUTERONOMY 4:9 CEV

I was recently invited to a garden party. The springtime garden was lovely, fragrant with the aroma of the cathedral of God's creation and vibrant with colorful blossoms of renewed life. Even the swooping, twittering blue jays seemed to celebrate the ethereal beauty and joy of the season.

A dozen of us old friends, linked for several decades by a mutual profession, gathered at the invitation of Beth, our hostess, in her well-tended backyard. The purpose of the gathering was to honor Marlene, who had recently been diagnosed with an aggressive malignant brain tumor.

Marlene, single and in her late fifties, knew she had little time left, but had never been one for mushy sentiment. Not prone to tip-toe around the truth, she was well known for her pragmatic, no-nonsense approach to, well, everything. In the twenty years I'd known her, I had always found Marlene's call-a-spade-a-spade blatancy amusing and most refreshing. But she was never dying before. What brutal honesty would this day hold?

I steeled my insides for a very tough good-bye.

After we'd picked demurely at various salads and fruit compotes, and wolfed down enough chocolate éclair cake to choke a mule, Marlene turned the tables on us completely. She announced that we were all to sit in a circle on Beth's patio to play Chinese gift exchange, a game that I had previously only experienced at Christmastime.

Puzzled, we protested that we hadn't brought gifts; what could we possibly exchange? No, Marlene assured us, it'll work out, you'll see.

So we reluctantly took our seats and Marlene had us all draw numbers from a hat that had recently adorned her chemo-induced, hairless head. In a surprise move even to our hostess, Marlene calmly brought out eleven of her own purses, which she arranged on the coffee table in the center of the room. We were each to choose one as Marlene's gift to us.

Now these were not new purses, but well-loved, cherished handbags that bore the fingerprints of Marlene's life. Some were dressy, some casual, others quirky, but all represented facets of Marlene's very self, the essence and spirit that made Marlene. . .Marlene. She had chosen each one specially and, without fuss or fanfare, wanted to give this little part of herself to her special friends.

We were stunned. The silence was broken by the chattering of a baby squirrel in the towering oak nearby.

A leaden lump formed in the back of my throat. I fought back tears. My first thoughts were: *I can't take a dying woman's purse! I simply won't do it. I won't!* I could see similar feelings reflected in the ashen faces of the others. Marlene had anticipated this response and halted our rising protests with one heart-wrenching sentence.

"Please. I want you to have them to remember me by."

I haven't yet been able to bring myself to use my navy clutch, even in honor of my friend. Instead it sits atop my dresser as a daily reminder of the fragility of life. That one day the legacy of each of us that remains in the lives of our friends and family will be all they have to remember us by.

What will that legacy be?

Will they remember a woman of beauty and grace, regardless of her sometimes haggard appearance? Or will that ugly inner beast—the times when ranting, raving, and roaring rip right past self-control—be what they recall most?

Will it be a preoccupied wife, mother, or friend always rushing off somewhere to accomplish never-ending tasks? A woman whose priorities were so skewed that she failed to put *people* before *things*? A frantic soul who missed out on living because she chose to wrestle life instead?

Or will it be the power of prayer, of unconditional love, of faith that floats even in the stress-pool of life? Will it be memories of a life well lived, moments savored, laughter shared? I hope that's what my legacy will be.

I pray it will be.

And more than just hoping and praying, that little blue purse on my dresser implores me to make it happen. To build my legacy brick by brick, experience by meaningful experience. To focus *now* on the impact my life has on others around me. . .my loved ones, my workmates, those I labor alongside at church, my neighbors. Even my casual acquaintances. I don't want to leave my legacy to chance, do you?

For once we are physically gone from this earth, how incredible it is to know that our legacy will go on. Not just during this generation but for generations to come. We can use that legacy to influence others toward or repel them from eternity with our Lord in heaven. We can choose to create the legacy of a beautiful, joyful, vibrant woman—*alive* in every sense of the word.

Or create the legacy of an ogre.

The choice truly is ours.

> *The legacy we leave is not just in our possessions,*
> *but in the quality of our lives.*
>
> BILLY GRAHAM

Taming the Beast

1. Do you have any possessions that remind you of the legacy of someone special?

2. What memories of yourself do you desire most to leave behind as your legacy?

3. Are there any changes you feel led to make in your life, ones that will help build the legacy you're hoping for?

Chapter 32
I've Got Your Back

(Encouraging Others)

Encourage one another and build each other up.

1 Thessalonians 5:11 NIV

My friend Terri didn't know what to do. Her husband had been out of work for four years, and to say finances were tight would be an understatement. School was about to start and summer had worn out her preteen son's sneakers. She combed thrift shops to no avail—where would she ever find affordable shoes for his hard-to-fit feet?

Terri's prayer group prayed specifically for this need and encouraged her to trust that God was on it.

Then on Friday, three days before school was to resume, Terri heard a knock at her door. There stood a neighbor boy, two years older than Terri's son. They were moving, he explained, and he'd been cleaning out his closet and came across these shoes. Could her son use them?

He held out a pair of sneakers *exactly* like the ones Terri had been searching for. Barely worn and in excellent condition. A perfect fit.

When Terri joyfully shared this story with me, I remembered another account of meeting friends' needs in Luke 5:17–24. When these motivated buds couldn't squeeze their paralyzed friend through the crowds surrounding Jesus, they went through major trouble hauling him up to the roof, where they opened up a hole (hope there was homeowners' insurance!) and, using ropes and a stretcher, lowered him right smack in front of Jesus.

202   More Beauty, Less Beast ::

"Seeing their faith, He said, 'Friend, your sins are forgiven you. . . . I say to you, get up, and pick up your stretcher and go home' " (Luke 5:20, 24 NASB).

Whoa! Did you catch that? This guy's life was permanently altered because of the faith of his proactive friends! Jesus saw *their* faith—not the faith of the man himself—and responded.

Yes, friends who encourage us are more than just a blessing. They're a lifeline directly to God's heart. *Their* faith on our behalf, especially when we're weak or discouraged, is the nerve that innervates the muscles in the hand of God. And their encouragement is often the very thing that keeps us going.

Okay, you may be thinking, *I want to help others like that. How do I become an encourager?*

This was a question I tackled seriously about fifteen years ago. I learned that if you ask Papa God to grow you into an encourager, He *will*, but the transformation doesn't happen overnight—it's definitely a journey, one of the most rewarding expeditions I've ever experienced. Begin your own encouragement adventure with these four traveling tips:

- See a need; do the deed. Like the paralytic's friends, our first step is to recognize someone's need. It may be physical; it may be emotional or spiritual. It may be overt or carefully hidden. But we can't help until we *see* his or her need, and to do that we must keep discerning eyes open. Intentionally look around. Ask the Lord to help you notice things about people. You might be surprised what suddenly becomes visible.

I've found that one of the best ways to encourage others is by

meeting their physical needs. I'm not talking megabucks for new cars or houses (although some people are financially blessed enough to offer these); in these tough economic times, most of us must carefully budget our generosity. Even a peanut butter sandwich is immensely appreciated when you're hungry.

When Papa God places someone's specific need on my heart, I slip him or her a small sum (anonymously, if possible) earmarked for gas, eyeglasses, dentures, groceries, clothing, or to help pay that worrisome bill. Even a few dollars given in love toward a specific need is a huge encouragement, evidence that someone really does care.

Giving doesn't always have to be about money, either. Because of the particular skill set God has given me, I've been able to assist an elderly lady in writing her memoir, help a disabled man fulfill a lifelong desire by teaching him how to play the piano, and give free therapy to an unemployed woman who broke both her arms. It's incredibly cool to share what you know with someone who needs just that.

How can you encourage someone through your unique gift set?

- Obey those holy jabs. One sunny July morning, while I was frantically running errands with only an hour to hit four stops, a thought infiltrated my preoccupied brain: *"Call Sandi."*

What? *Nah.* I'd just spoken with my girlfriend two days earlier and she was enjoying summer freedom from her teaching job. Why should I bother her? I mentally deleted the message as I ran into the crowded post office.

But the nagging nudge just wouldn't go away, like an invisible elbow jabbing my side. *"Call Sandi,"* I heard at the bank. *"Call Sandi,"*

in the deli line. "She's fine!" I countered, still thinking I was arguing with myself and not the Almighty. Finally, in one of my least impressive spiritual moments, I rolled my eyes and grudgingly entered Sandi's number in my cell phone, muttering, "Oh, for heaven's sake. Like I have time for this."

Then I suddenly realized that the persistent message truly *was* for heaven's sake when Sandi answered sobbing. I could barely understand her. She'd just received a call that one of her beloved young students had unexpectedly died, and she was home alone, completely distraught. I did a U-turn and headed straight to Sandi's house, humbled but grateful that I could be there to support my friend.

What if I had ignored that little voice dogging me? What if I'd decided I was too busy to make that call? Or that it wasn't convenient? I would have never received the amazing blessing of being my Father's "daughter of encouragement" (like Barnabas, the "son of encouragement" in Acts 4:36–37 [NIV]).

- Be willing. Like the paralytic's friends, who were willing to give their time, effort, and resources to encourage their friend, we need to be willing to dig deep, too. In helping dig someone out of his or her troubles, we're often providing a hole to bury our own. Even if it means interrupting our own busy schedules for an unexpected development.

Girl, I gotta tell you—this is a major struggle for me. As a planner by nature, interruptions chafe my hiney. I must constantly remind myself that the Good Samaritan (see Luke 10:30–37), our example of a man helping someone in need, willingly stopped mid-journey and instantly altered his entire itinerary to assist a stranger.

Ugh. Just shoot me. I've never been very schedule-flexible. I'm way too production-oriented and often—I hate to admit this—delegate people to the rear of the priority bus. *Bad*, Debbie! I know, I know. But I'm determined to learn to bend like a metal rod beneath my Master Welder's blowtorch. Even if it kills me. And it might.

Is being an encourager exhausting? Exasperating? Inconvenient? Sometimes. Okay, lots of times. But I've found that if I'm willing to go the extra mile, God will provide the gasoline.

- Become a cheerleader. With my one-inch vertical leap, I could never be a high school cheerleader like such notables as Ronald Reagan, Samuel L. Jackson, George W. Bush, Paula Abdul, Halle Berry, Steve Martin (yup, I can picture that!), Madonna, Jimmy Stewart, and—believe it or not—Ruth Bader Ginsburg. (Pause to snicker here.)

But being an encourager is a different type of cheerleading— it's actively listening to someone's worries, offering tenderness and acceptance, and reflecting the hope of Christ to one who may never meet Him in church. "But encourage one another day after day, as long as it is still called 'Today'" (Hebrews 3:13 NASB).

Ironically, in this age of bustling busyness, time can be the most difficult but also the most inspiring form of encouragement we can give. Sometimes people need our undivided attention and physical presence to reaffirm their identity and personal worth. We act as God's love in a tangible form when we yield ourselves to allow His love to flow through us to hurting people.

Touch is an underutilized way to give others a priceless lift. Little hugs to an elderly neighbor for no reason except to say, "You're special

to me." A thirty-second shoulder rub to the frazzled secretary to express how valued she is; that unexpected evening foot massage for your exhausted spouse; a sympathetic squeeze to the hand of a friend venting her frustration about her new boss.

Just think how much caring human touch cheers your heart when you're down. That's cheerleading at its finest. There's nothing simpler or more effective that we can do to boost someone's spirit. Touch heals. I've seen it time and time again in my role as a therapist. Our Creator wired us to crave touch—there's a reason it's one of our five basic senses. We *need* touch. Not only to receive it, but to give it.

Does being an encourager carry a price tag? Yes, indeed. It can cost us precious time, limited funds, our own urgent agendas, plus tons of physical and emotional energy. Is the expense worth it? Absolutely! "The one who blesses others is abundantly blessed; those who help others are helped" (Proverbs 11:25 MSG). When we encourage others, we can't help but be encouraged ourselves. By making someone else's little world more beautiful, ours becomes more beautiful, too.

Mother Teresa (did you know her real name was Agnes Gonxha Bojarhiu?) said, "There are many in the world who are dying for a piece of bread, but there are many more dying for a little love."

Pssst. That's the sound of the whizzing arrow hitting your heart.

So when someone's at the end of her rope and you feel the tug, go ahead, sister. Offer your hand. Share a piece of God's beauty from your heart. And then grab your hacksaw and start cutting a hole in the roof.

Unless someone like you cares a whole awful lot,
nothing is going to get better. It's not.

Dr. Seuss

Taming the Beast

1. Can you remember when someone's encouragement carried you through a time of need?
2. Do you think it's important for followers of Christ to encourage others?
3. Can you think of one person in your life for whom you're willing to go the extra mile to encourage right now? How and when will you do it?

CHAPTER 33
The Real Thing
(Preparing for Heaven)

What you hope for is kept safe for you in heaven.

COLOSSIANS 1:5 CEV

Ever had a near brush with death? I must say it certainly casts everyday trivial pursuits in a new perspective. Especially when it happens twice in one hour.

It was the final day of my He & Me Retreat last summer (yep, the very one from chapter 10). I'd spent five glorious days alone in a Smoky Mountain cabin, savoring some major face time with Papa God. About midafternoon, I decided to make the trek down the mountain to check my e-mail and do a little shopping.

Setting up my laptop at a cozy table in a little chocolate shop, I spent nearly an hour answering e-mail and people-watching through the big picture window. I reflected on the wonderful week I'd had immersing myself in the Word and connecting with Jesus in a deeper, more intimate way than I had in a long time. My heart felt full to overflowing.

About the time I headed back to my car, ominous clouds began rolling in and the sky turned the color of bruises. *Oh man,* I thought. *Hope this storm holds off a little longer. I need to stop at the grocery store and pick up something for dinner or I'll be eating canned corn tonight.*

Just as I pulled into the grocery store parking lot, the sky split wide open. I grabbed my umbrella from the backseat floorboard, tucked my purse against my chest, and sprinted (now mind you, sprinting for me would be considered jogging for most folks) toward the store entrance with my umbrella low and angled against the rain blowing in from my left side.

As I crossed the expanse directly in front of the store, thinking only about the puddles soaking my sandaled feet, I heard the sickening screech of car tires but my view was blocked by the umbrella. A woman standing in the store entrance screamed and pointed in my direction as I involuntarily braced myself. . .for what, I didn't know. Suddenly, entering my field of vision beneath the canopy of my umbrella, was the front bumper of a car as it skidded to a stop on the wet asphalt, shiny chrome coming to rest snugly against my left hip.

Only then did I realize the full impact of my near impact. I could have easily been run down. I laid my left hand on the car's hood, which was nudging my now-trembling body, and lifted my umbrella to see the horrified face of the driver, his hand flying to his forehead as he exhaled a long, relieved breath.

Not knowing what else to do, I continued on to the store entrance, where comments flew from the half-dozen shocked onlookers gathered there.

"Good heavens, lady, you were almost killed!"

"What was that guy doing driving that fast in a downpour?"

"Doesn't he know pedestrians have the right of way in front of a store?"

"Your guardian angel must've been flying low today, ma'am!"

As I stood there in mute shock, the store's electricity flickered, then died. Pretty much how my insides felt. Although I was shaking so hard I was afraid my knees might buckle at any moment, all I could think of was getting back to my warm, safe cabin, dinner or no dinner.

So back through the cold rain I dashed, collapsing over the steering wheel when I finally sloshed into the driver's seat and slammed the door behind me.

Okay. I'm okay. Just breathe in and out. Thank You, Lord; You saved my life. Or at the very least, a long night at the emergency room. After a few tears trickled and I'd offered up another heartfelt prayer of gratitude, I cranked my car and began the tedious ascent up the mountain in the torrential rain.

The trip to our cabin, up the winding, narrow road flanked by sheer drops, normally takes twenty-five minutes. But it was taking twice as long in that horrible thunderstorm with dusk closing in. About halfway up, hail began pounding my windshield and I slowed to 15 mph, barely able to make out the center line as visibility decreased to almost nil.

Rounding a sharp curve, I was startled to see, in a timely flash of lightning, an enormous tree falling across the road directly in front of my car, crushing the smaller trees and brush in its path. Thankfully, I was moving slowly because of the weather and was able to brake just in time with only minimal fishtailing. I sat staring at the massive trunk and heavy limbs sprawled across the exact spot where my car would have been if I'd gotten there five seconds earlier.

Five seconds. The difference between life and death. . .the finite and infinity.

After some kindhearted men in pickups worked together to tie ropes on the fallen tree and drag it aside enough to clear one lane, I was on my way. When I finally arrived back at the cabin, the storm had passed. I was restless and needed desperately to feel Papa God's calming embrace. I clipped on Fenway's leash and together we walked down to the meadow filled with baby Christmas trees, all lined up in their young, fresh-smelling splendor. I enjoyed watching them grow, knowing they were fulfilling their destiny of bringing cheer and festivity into someone's living room one day.

Instead of the smile the little fir trees usually elicited, I found myself feeling sad over their impending doom. They had been cultivated and planted only to die, to be cut down in their prime, trussed up, and trucked to some faraway location to be enjoyed for a short season and then discarded and burned like useless kindling.

Odd, the twist in perspective that had occurred since my own near demise that afternoon. Life suddenly seemed very fragile—a whisper in the wind, a daisy wilting in the field, a fawn downed by an errant gunshot. Death seemed to loom so much closer, as threatening and foreboding as the dark storm clouds that had precipitated my frightening experiences.

Born to die. . .something about that phrase tugged at my memory as I wandered through the Christmas tree farm. Where had I heard that before?

Oh yes. It was the description of Christ that my pastor had used in church several weeks before. Jesus Christ, the Son of God, was born to die, like the little trees before me. Christ's sole purpose in taking on human form, in being born as a sweet flesh-and-blood Babe in a manger, was to eventually die. To be the payment, the blood sacrifice for our sins.

Fresh tears stung my eyes as I recognized anew this incredible thing Jesus had done for me. And because of His infinite love and His willingness to die in my place, everlasting life is mine. "For God so loved the world that He gave His only begotten Son, that whoever believes in Him should not perish but have everlasting life" (John 3:16 NKJV).

And not only was He willing to sacrifice Himself in my stead—and yours—He took great pleasure in providing for us His way, His truth, and His life (see John 14:6), our *only* possible way to heaven. He bridged the gap between this life and the next with Himself, not because we could ever do anything to deserve it, but because He wanted to share eternity with us.

Getting into heaven isn't graded on the curve; we don't get there by being better than someone else. We get there by faith alone. . .in Christ alone. . .by grace alone.

"Even before he made the world, God loved us and chose us in Christ to be holy and without fault in his eyes. God decided in advance to adopt us into his own family by bringing us to himself through Jesus Christ. This is what he wanted to do, and it gave him great pleasure" (Ephesians 1:4–5 NLT).

If we receive His precious gift of salvation, we don't have to fear death, dear friend. It's merely a door opening to the greatest adventure of all: heaven! After all, Jesus left home so that we could find it.

Faith is like radar that sees through the fog.
CORRIE TEN BOOM

Taming the Beast

1. Have you ever had a near-death experience? Or loved someone who has? How did it make you feel about the fragility of life and eternity?

2. Have you made your reservation in heaven? Did you know Jesus has a seat beside Him at His table with your name on it? He *wants* to spend time with you, beautiful sister.

3. If you haven't already received the amazing gift of salvation, accept it now. If you have, thank Papa God for the new adventure you have to look forward to.

Chapter 34
Transforming the Ogre

(Living Beautifully)

Let the king be enthralled by your beauty;
honor him, for he is your lord.

PSALM 45:11 NIV

So we've reached the end of our quest to discover God's standard of beauty, and I hope you've gotten as much out of our search as I have. I think the most important concept to take away from this book is this:

People love makeovers, but God loves transformations.

And once the transformation process has begun, He wants us to see ourselves as beautiful as He sees us. In fact, according to the scripture above, He will be *enthralled* by our beauty! *Enthralled!* That means charmed, fascinated, held spellbound. Whoa—who else in this whole wide world can we say is so absolutely smitten with us?

All the time we spend looking in the mirror, primping, adjusting, and reinventing ourselves, will be for naught if we're not beautified from the inside out. If that hideous beast within is not dealt with, it *will* emerge during times of emotional crisis and destroy everything good, everything lovely, everything beautiful in our lives with its vicious, relentless claws.

But Papa God equips us not only to fight the beast, but to subdue it permanently—our whip is His Word, our chair is the Holy Spirit's power, and the lock on the cage is laughter. Author Ann Spangler said, "She who laughs, lasts." So true.

When that inner beast growls and rattles your cage with everyday chaos, what can you do to shut its ugly face? Laugh. That's right, laugh! Out loud! And you might also try my three favorite stress relievers:

1. Nyquil on the rocks (the alcohol in Geritol gives you too much of a buzz)
2. Cracking nuts with a sledgehammer (oh-so satisfying)
3. Shredding old newspapers barehanded (who needs a machine?)

Listen, life doesn't have to be a hard, tooth-jarring journey. Barbara Johnson said, "Laughter is to life what shock absorbers are to automobiles. It won't take the potholes out of the road, but it sure makes the ride smoother."

So these are my final words of beautifying near-wisdom to share with you:

- When the jeans on your attitude are tight, unbutton and take a deep breath, girl!
- Say this aloud every day: "I am more than a number on a scale."
- Makeup, hairstyles, and clothes hold power. *If* we let them. Don't.
- Color your world with the crayons God gives you. Beauty is just a shade away.

My prayer for you, dear sister, is that you will realize how *enthralling* your unique beauty truly is to the only One who counts: your Father, the King! Allow Him to transform that ugly inner beast into the beautiful princess you were meant to be! May your life be filled with joy, love, and fulfillment. (And barrels of Godiva!)

Notes

1 "Obesity's Price Higher for Women," *The Tampa Tribune*, September 21, 2010, 12.

2 "Fat Is Burden as Women Age," *The Tampa Tribune*, September 30, 2009, 17.

3 "Bulging Belly Increases Risk of Death," *The Tampa Tribune*, August 10, 2010, 15.

4 "Hour a Day Keeps Flab Away," *The Tampa Tribune*, March 24, 2010, 14.

5 "Exercise Tackles Cancer," *The Tampa Tribune*, June 29, 2010, 13.

6 "Wellness Watch," *Mind Body Sole*, Fall 2010, 4.

7 Ibid.

8 Emily Listfield, "Apps to Keep You Fit," *Parade*, October 2010.

9 Madison Park, "Twinkie Diet Helps Nutrition Professor Lose 27 Pounds," CNN.com, November 8, 2010.

10 James W. Goll, "When You Have Done All," *Charisma*, October 2010, 45–48.

[11] John & Stasi Eldredge, "Love Is a Battlefield," *Homelife*, August 2010, 28–30.

[12] Ray Reyes, "Stressed Out: Forbes Ranks Tampa No. 4," *Tampa Tribune*, August 18, 2010, 6.

[13] Kristen Reed, "Federal Prison? It's Not So Bad," *Orlando Sentinel*, January 9, 2007, 12.

[14] The Monkees recorded "Daydream Believer" by John Stewart on June 14, 1967, and August 9, 1967; the song appears on *The Birds, the Bees & the Monkees*; No. 1 Billboard single in December 1967.

[15] Marie Armenia, "The Roller-Coaster Male," *Homelife*, June 2010, 28.

Visit with the Author

Deb would love to chat with you and even share a few nuggets of her own offbeat brand of wit and near-wisdom with your church or women's group. Befriend her on Facebook and Twitter, and keep in touch through her website and blogs: www.DeboraCoty.com.

LOOK FOR THESE FAITH-INSPIRING BOOKS BY DEBORA M. COTY:

Too Blessed to Be Stressed
Inspiration for Climbing Out of Life's Stress-Pool

If you're searching for peace in your frazzled heart, hope for a better tomorrow, and a smile for your stress-creased face, you'll cherish this healthy dose of truth gift-wrapped in humor. Sometimes every woman needs a life preserver in the churning everyday stress-pool.

365 Chick-isms:
Witty Musings on Life, Love, and Laughter

A wonderful gift book of daily fun, near-wisdom, and chick-chat for those beloved women in your life.

Everyday Hope

A lovely, feminine collection of 200 short devotions that replenish and encourage in the soul-lifting hope of the Master Creator. A delightful gift for friends and family who need a fresh touch of everlasting hope for everyday life!

Prayers for Daughters

Power-packed short prayers expressing the fears, joys, and hopes of girls aged 8 to 18. Adorable gift books for those special girls in your life who would benefit from a delicious daily spiritual vitamin.

Scripture Index